Series / Number 07-055

THE LOGIC OF CAUSAL ORDER

JAMES A. DAVIS
Harvard University

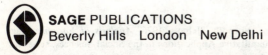

SAGE PUBLICATIONS
Beverly Hills   London   New Delhi

For information address:

SAGE Publications, Inc.
275 South Beverly Drive
Beverly Hills, California 90212

SAGE Publications Inc.
2111 West Hillcrest Drive
Newbury Park
California 91320

SAGE Publications Ltd.
28 Banner Street
London EC1Y 8QE
England

SAGE PUBLICATIONS India Pvt. Ltd.
M-32 Market
Greater Kailash I
New Delhi 110 048 India

International Standard Book Number 0-8039-2553-0

Library of Congress Catalog Card No. 85-062371

FOURTH PRINTING, 1988

When citing a university paper, please use the proper form. Remember to cite the correct
Sage University Paper series title and include the paper number. One of the following
formats can be adapted (depending on the style manual used):

(1) IVERSEN, GUDMUND R. and NORPOTH, HELMUT (1976) "Analysis of
Variance." Sage University Paper series on Quantitative Applications in the Social
Sciences, 07-001. Beverly Hills: Sage Pubns.

OR

(2) Iversen, Gudmund R. and Norpoth, Helmut. 1976. *Analysis of Variance.* Sage
University Paper series on Quantitative Applications in the Social Sciences, series no.
07-001. Beverly Hills: Sage Pubns.

CONTENTS

Series Editor's Introduction

In the explosive growth of social science statistical methods, it is easy to forget that quantitative research rests on logical foundations that cut across specific techniques. Which is the dependent variable? Which variables shall we control? Would a change in X produce as much change in Y as the coefficient implies?

The answers to these questions are not purely statistical. This is not to say that the answers are arbitrary or whimsical. Over the years the research community has developed a repertoire of maxims such as "never control on a dependent variable," or "the correlation is explained if the partial coefficient goes down to zero." In the early post-World War II era Lazarsfeld's "logic of survey analysis" provided a synthesis of sorts. But three decades have passed, and the classic formulations are no longer sufficient. Yet contemporary methodologists seldom pause to explain their prestatistical assumptions in nontechnical language.

In this monograph Professor Davis, himself a veteran survey analyst, spells out some of these logical principles that underlie our collective wisdom and rules of thumb. The central notion in this paper is "causal direction." Professor Davis defines it and explains how the practical researcher posits directionality. He then shows how the notion can be extended from pairs of variables to larger systems. Having defined the key ideas, he shows how they are used in statistical analysis in the social sciences: rules for deciding what variables to control, the causal interpretations of various calculations, and the reasoning behind "elaboration," "effects analysis," and "path analysis."

This monograph is not statistical in the sense of developing specific statistical tools. Rather, it explains the prestatistical assumptions required, whatever the technique. The book stresses the importance of substantive knowledge about the "real world" and repeatedly challenges the myth that causal problems can be solved by statistical calculations alone. The latter assumption has crept into the work of second- and third-generation "causal modelers," although the founders of causal modeling in the social sciences, including Hubert Blalock, specifically warned against such a fallacy. Professor Davis shows us that in spite of our best efforts to avoid the tendency to fall back on technique, collectively we will fail unless periodically we are reminded of the dangers associated with an exaggerated reliance on statistical solutions to extrastatistical problems. We are delighted to add the pedagogic skills of Professor Davis to the QASS series of methodology monographs.

—John L. Sullivan
Series Co-Editor

THE LOGIC OF CAUSAL ORDER

JAMES A. DAVIS
Harvard University

1. INTRODUCTION

This book is about statistical analysis of social science data, but it isn't about statistics. It is about something much more important: how to think about your research problem so you can ask the right questions with your statistics. Once you have posed the right questions, the choice of a language (multiple regression, loglinear effects, percentage tables, analysis of variance, etc.) is a secondary problem. Secondary doesn't mean trivial: Choice of technique is an important part of the craft of research. But secondary does mean next in importance. Seasoned research workers know every legitimate statistical scheme will give you just about the same answer to such key questions as, "Is this variable really strongly related to that one?" or "Which of these variables has the weakest effect?" But no statistical routine can give you the right answer if you choose the wrong variables to analyze.

If you think of each particular statistical analysis (e.g., estimating a multiple regression coefficient or constructing a cross-tabulation) as "making a run," the prior questions are, "Which variables shall I include in this run? Shall I run X against Y or Y against X? Should I control for *this*? And if I control for *this*, must I also control for *that*?" No statistics text or user's guide will tell you the answers. In part, this is because the answers depend on substantive, empirical matters—the more you know about social stratification, presidential voting, job satisfaction, or whatever, the easier it will be to plan your run. But there is more to it than knowledge of the merchandise. You also use *logical* rules that

AUTHOR'S NOTE: *"Thank yous" being in order, I'd like to express mine to Garth Taylor, who corrected a humbling number of errors in the first draft. Regrettably, neither of us can guarantee he got them all.*

apply across every content area, the rules that are spelled out in this book.

These rules are about *causal order* in a set of variables—assumptions about which is the "cause" and which is the "effect" when you look at the relationship between two variables. For example, if you were studying the relationship between income and political party preference, without even reading this book, you'd naturally assume income was the "cause" and party was the "effect." This book helps you think through the unstated reasons that led you to your choice and see what follows when you make such assumptions for every pair of variables in your analysis.

Oddly enough, the crucial principles are seldom written down, possibly because many seem so obvious (e.g., "something afterwards can't cause something that happened before it"), possibly because some of them (e.g., the very concept "cause") raise weighty philosophical problems if pushed too far.

Instead, the principles exist as a sort of unwritten folklore young scientists learn by osmosis; that is, by imitating their elders. The point of this book is to get these ideas down on paper and show you how to use them in your research decisions. I will use examples from textbook statistics, but with one exception (path analysis), the ideas are not tied to any particular calculations.

So, unlike the other books in this series, this is not a statistics text. But it isn't a philosophy text either. Many of the formulations will look terribly informal to a philosopher of science, and at least one, "causation," is a notorious philosophical tar pit. One of the important principles of the philosophy of science is that the working scientist depends on formulations that don't quite hold water under the scrutiny of a professional philosopher. Thus, the ideas I will spell out are the unspoken assumptions of the professional social science researcher, not the honed formulations of the professional logician.

What does the book actually cover? We begin with the notion of causal direction and the principles to use when you decide that X is the cause of Y instead of the other way around. Then we see how—when you have made such directional assumptions for each pair in a collection of variables—the collection of variables may be viewed as a causal *system*.

The notion of "system" is one of the key concepts in modern social research. Here, at least, we go beyond the vague assumption that "everything is involved with everything else" to develop three ideas: (1) the idea of *indirect* effects; (2) the idea of *causally spurious* effects; and (3) the idea of *signed* effects. The three ideas, taken together, provide a rich and exact way to discuss the fascinating and complex ripples of causation that make even the smallest multivariate systems fascinating.

Having laid out the vocabulary and principles of ordered causal systems, we then shift to the ways in which the research worker uses them to "set up a run." The central notion is "control" and the central problem is when and when not to introduce variables as controls. The issue is "whether," not "how." "How" is explained in statistics texts; "whether" depends on your assumptions about causal order. There is actually a straightforward answer (see Rule #7 in the Appendix if you are dying of curiosity), but it can be applied in either simple or complicated (rich) ways. Thus, we end the book with a Chinese box of analysis strategies ranging from the very simple idea of "elaboration" to the complex and sophisticated technique called "path analysis." Each, however, is nothing more than the application of Rule #7 in a plain or fancy way.

The "paradox" of all this is this: Although assumptions about causal order are vital for nonexperimental research, they can seldom be checked nonexperimentally. (The relevance of the logic for controlled experiments is discussed in the section on control.) Therefore, it behooves us to consider prayerfully how much damage is done when our assumptions are, in fact, wrong. This book ends on this sobering, but far from despondent, note.

Two Variables

Variable X is a cause of Variable Y when

—Change in X (sooner or later) produces change in Y
—or (because some Xs don't change) Ys tend to line up with fixed values of X.

Examples:

Employment is a cause of earnings: People who get (lose) jobs increase (decrease) their earnings.

Marital status is a cause of sociability patterns: When people get married they cut their frequency of visits to bars and taverns.

Race is a cause of party: Blacks are more likely to become Democrats than are whites.

Education is a cause of occupational prestige: People who hold college degrees are more likely to get high-status jobs.

With such sophisticated readers, I hardly need add:

(1) We are talking about "averages" or "tendencies." Individual exceptions are to be expected.

(2) To say "X is a cause of Y" is not to say "X is *the* cause of Y."

(3) Correlation alone doesn't prove causation. (This book is devoted to what else you need.)

(4) Nonexperimental data of the sort treated in this book are less persuasive evidence than appropriately controlled experiments (but a lot more persuasive than casual observation, anecdotes, folk lore, TV talk show hosts, or professors' opinions).

Social research aims to develop causal propositions supported by data and logic. The principles of statistics and probability provide part of the logic, but not all of it. In addition, research workers draw on a more general "logic of causal systems" that applies to diverse statistical schemes. The core of this logic is the notion of "causal order."

For the two variables, X and Y, we distinguish among four possibilities. Each has a conventional symbol using arrows:

(1) X⟶Y   X might influence Y but Y does not influence X.

(2) Y⟵X   Y might influence X but X does not influence Y.

(3) X⇄Y   X and Y might influence each other.

(4) X⟷Y   X and Y might show statistical coordination (correlation), but for present purposes I do not assume anything about direction.

The word "might" appears in each formulation. It is not necessary to know that X *does* cause Y, it is only necessary that causation is conceivable or possible. Thus an arrow indicates *potential* flows of causation, not necessarily actual flows. The situation is like a street map indicating one-way streets. It does not tell us whether there are any cars on the streets; but if there are any, it tells us which way they can move.

Case 3 and Case 4 look similar at first glance, but they are sharply different. In Case 3 causal influence can go both ways. (Mothers who have additional children tend to cut back their hours of work. Mothers who decide to take on full-time jobs are likely to postpone additional babies.) Case 4 is entirely different. It says the true situation could be "any of the above" or even "none of the above" (if neither influences the other), but in this analysis I will dodge the question.

The differences among Cases 1, 2, and 3 turn on the notion of *impossible* (well, exceedingly improbable) causal flows. Thus, we run the arrow from X to Y if it is possible that X might influence Y but impossible for Y to influence X. Consider, for example, X = neatness of one's room at college and Y = becoming president of the United States. It is possible (although hardly probable) that people with neat rooms have a greater chance of becoming president, but there is no way that incumbency in the White House can influence tidiness back in college days.

How can you tell that a causal flow is impossible? You can't to the satisfaction of someone who just got an A– in "Introduction to Philosophy." But for the purposes of research, scientists apply several plausible, although not infallible, rules.

The rules have nothing to do with statistics. Although the methodological journals teem with crackpot proposals for determining causal order using only the numbers in the data set, most methodologists agree that causal order is a substantive or empirical problem to be solved by our knowledge about how the real world works, not by statistical gyrations. At the philosophical level this has positive and negative implications. On the negative side, empirical research is always hostage to empirical assumptions that might be wrong; on the positive side, computers cannot substitute for sociologists in analyzing data, because computers do not know anything about the real world and sociologists do know a little bit.

I will lay out four rules, but each is really only a special application of the great principle of causal order: *after cannot cause before* . . . there is no way to change the past . . . one-way arrows flow with time.

It is also helpful to think of a variable as having "start" and "freeze" dates. The start date is the date before which no score can exist, the freeze date is the date after which no change in score is possible.

Consider, for example, the question "Did you serve in the Armed Forces in World War II? Yes or No." The variable has a start date of 1941 and a freeze date of 1946. Before 1941 the question couldn't be asked, and after 1946 everyone must remain in the category (yes or no) in which he or she was at the end of the war.

Variables may or may not have clear cut start and freeze dates. When they do, Rule 1a applies:

Rule 1a: Run the arrow from X to Y if Y starts after X freezes.

Thus, for example, one would run arrows:

From	To
service in World War II ⟶	attitudes toward the Vietnam war
football victories in the fall ⟶	alumni gifts the following June
the recession in 1974 and 1975 ⟶	election results in 1976

In each case, scores on Y didn't even begin until after X scores were frozen. There were no attitudes toward Vietnam in 1946, the football statistics were entered into the record books months before alumni decisions were made, the 1975 recession was over before the 1976 elections began.

Note: Anticipation of Y may precede the freeze date for X (e.g., the president may try to influence the economy because of an upcoming election), but the anticipation of Y is a different variable than Y. It may be studied and included in a system like this:

$$\text{(Anticipation of Y)} \longrightarrow \text{(X)} \longrightarrow \text{(Y)}$$

But Y still follows X. There is no way an actual outcome, Y, can cause its anticipation; anticipations may be dead wrong.

Actual dates are handy, but not strictly necessary if X and Y can be tied to a sequence of events such that later stages cannot occur until earlier ones have been completed.

Rule 1b: Run the arrow from X to Y if X is linked to an earlier step in a well-known sequence.

Thus:

prestige of first job ⟶	prestige of second job
SAT scores in high school ⟶	college grades
preference in the primary election ⟶	preference in the general election

The life cycle is a sequence sociologists use frequently. The steps are not perfect (some people do have babies and then get married—but very few), although the following sequence is fairly noncontroversial:

(1) characteristics of one's family "when you were growing up" (e.g., father's occupation);

(2) completion of formal schooling;

(3) first full-time job;

(4) first marriage;

(5) birth of children;

(6) dissolution of marriage by death or divorce.

Consequently, one would *not* submit research proposals to study

the influence of divorce (6) on age at first marriage (4);

the influence of fertility (5) on mother's educational attainment (1).

As parents and offspring go through similar life cycles but at staggered times, you can always run arrows from a parental step to the same or later step for their children. Thus, the following are plausible causal orders:

the influence of parents' schooling (2) on their children's schooling (2);

the influence of parents' fertility (5) on children's fertility (5);

the influence of parental education (2) on children's divorce (6).

Arrows for influence of a parental step on children's *earlier* step require some factual knowledge. Although it is common to study the influence of parental fertility (5) on offspring's schooling (2), the first child in a large family may complete schooling before his or her mother's age of possible fertility (usually assumed to be 15-49) ends.

It is not pure coincidence that sociologists have done so much research on "intergenerational mobility" and "parental influences on children's achievements." Such variables provide interesting and plausible channels for one-way causal flows. Indeed, the main statistical technique we use (path analysis of multiple regression coefficients) was invented by a geneticist (Sewall Wright) who was interested in the flow of genes through generations of guinea pigs.

A third rule applies when one of the variables is fixed and cannot change. Consider, for example, sex (gender). Clearly, sex is causal for many important sociological variables: attitudes, labor force participation, earnings, personality, media usage, and so on. But we hardly suggest (except to get sniggers in a bored classroom) that persons who change their sex tend to change their income. What do we assume? In the lingo of this chapter, I'd analyze it this way, using earnings and sex as examples:

Sex is fixed at birth and has a freeze date at age zero.

Earnings have various start dates, but they are all well after age zero.

Consequently, the start date for earnings follows the freeze date for sex and the arrow runs

sex→earnings

The case of a constant is really just an application of Rule 1a, but it is important enough to justify a special statement.

Rule 1c: If (during some span of time) X never changes and Y sometimes changes, run the arrow from X to Y. If neither X nor Y can change, use a double headed arrow.

Among the chief "constants" for studies of U.S. adults are sex, birth cohort (year of birth, not chronological age), race, and national origin.

There is one more principle. It is used every day, but I include it with some hesitation as it is prone to abuse. It goes like this:

Rule 1d: If X is relatively *stable, hard to change,* or *fertile,*[1] while Y is relatively *volatile, easy to change,* or *has few consequences,* run the arrow from X to Y.

Consider, for example, size of place (e.g., metropolitan versus rural) and favorite TV program. You and I would both run the arrow

size of place ⟶ TV program

Strictly speaking, the previous rules do not apply. Neither variable has a clear start or freeze date. Neither is part of a sequence, neither is a constant. However, we arrived at the same conclusion because we both (probably) reasoned like this:

> Although people do move from city to city, they don't do it very often and when they do, it is a fertile event.

> Although people do have favorite TV programs, they probably change frequently, such shifts are "cheap," and shifting does not lead to much.

> So, because city size is so sticky and favorite TV programs so loose, one can imagine that after moving, a person might shift TV preference, but it is hard to imagine anyone shifting communities on the basis of viewing habits.

Our argument seems plausible—at least to me—but it is not based on a shred of hard evidence. Nevertheless, sociologists proceed this way every day, and informal consensus has developed on many sticky and loose variables. Thus:

Relatively Sticky	*Relatively Loose*
(Xs)	*(Ys)*
religious preference	presidential popularity
religiosity (e.g., church attendance)	happiness, morale
occupational prestige	stands on political issues
size of place	media habits
region of residence	preference for candidates
national party identification	brand preference
IQ	
marital status	
household composition	

In summary, before statistical analysis of X and Y begins, we must think through our assumptions about causal order—whether we assume it is one-way, two-way, or undetermined. We run one-way arrows from X to Y if it is inconceivable that Y influences X but conceivable that X influences Y. Causal order cannot be determined by statistical gyrations. Instead, we use real world knowledge about the variable and four principles that are variations on the theme "after cannot cause before":

16

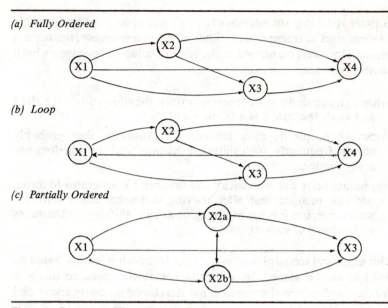

Figure 1   Examples of Four-Variable Systems

Run the arrow from X to Y if

(1a) Y starts after X freezes;

(1b) X is linked to an earlier step in a well-known sequence;

(1c) X never changes and Y sometimes changes;

(1d) X is more stable, harder to change, or more fertile.

SYSTEMS: ORDERED, BLOCK, AND LOOP

With three or more variables we have a system or network. To keep things straight and gain an intellectual purchase on what's going on, analysts use pictograms ("flow graphs," "path diagrams") in which variables are represented as dots or circles and their relationships by arrows, as in Figure 1.

At first glance the three systems in Figure 1 look the same. However, they differ in whether the four variables can be arranged in a neat sequence from first to last.

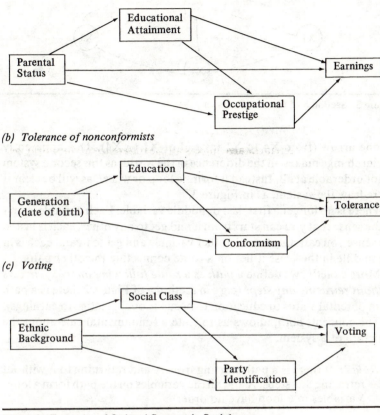

(a) Socioeconomic status (SES)

(b) Tolerance of nonconformists

(c) Voting

Figure 2 Examples of Ordered Systems in Sociology

The variables in section a form a complete order, X1 is first, X2 is second, X3 is third, and X4 is fourth and last. (Note, X4 has three incoming arrows, X3 has two, X2 has one, and X1 has zero. In a system in which all pairs are linked by a one-way arrow the variables will always be fully ordered if each has a different total of incoming arrows.)

Figure 2 shows examples of four variable ordered systems common in sociology.

Section b of Figure 1 illustrates a different causal structure, a loop. Section b is identical to section a *except* for the seemingly minor reversal

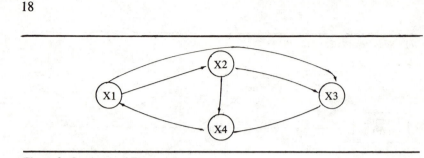

Figure 3   Section b of Figure 1 Redrawn

of one arrow (from X4 to X1 instead of X1 to X4). This apparently trivial change makes all the difference in the world, as this second system is not orderable at all. Instead it forms a loop or wheel, as will be clear if we redraw the system, as in Figure 3.

There is no longer a first, last or middle variable. Each variable is first in the sense that you can start from it and get to any other, each is last in the sense you can start from another variable and get to it, and each is in the middle in the sense it lies on a route connecting the other pairs.

More exactly, we define a *path* as a *route following one-way arrows without retracing any steps* (e.g., in section a of Figure 2 there is a path from parental status to education to occupational prestige to earnings).

The concept, *path*, allows us to state a fundamental rule about the structure of a system.

Rule 2: If there is a path starting from X and returning to it without retracing any steps, X and all the variables on the path form a loop. Variables in a loop have no order.

Loops have a triple importance:

Theoretically, in systems analysis loops magnify or dampen the effects when their variables influence one another.

Logically, they make it difficult to find an order for the variables.

Technically, loops create complicated statistical problems—so complicated that looped variables cannot be analyzed except by very sophisticated techniques *and* by invoking strong empirical assumptions about causal effects of outside variables feeding into the loop. (For a detailed explanation of this see Heise [1975] and Berry [1984].)

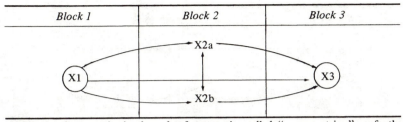

| Block 1 | Block 2 | Block 3 |

NOTE: In the quantitative branch of economics called "econometrics," perfectly ordered systems such as section a of Figure 1 are called "recursive" and systems such as section c are called "block recursive."

Figure 4   Section c of Figure 1 Redrawn as Ordered Blocks

The variables in section a of Figure 1 form a perfect order, whereas the variables in section b have no order at all. Those in section c are in between. X1 is clearly the first, X3 is clearly the last, and X2a and X2b are between them. However, we cannot decide whether X2a or X2b comes first, because they have a double-headed arrow. Such systems are called "partial orders" or "ordered blocks" because we can arrange the variables in groups or blocks and the blocks form an order. Figure 4 redraws section c of Figure 1 to illustrate.

Block systems can be very handy. We will soon see techniques that enable us to analyze them without the complexities of loop analyses or the dubious claim that each and every variable in the data has a unique place in a causal chain.

Data involving spouses frequently form block systems. One of the classic findings in sociology is that husbands and wives tend to resemble each other in terms of education, religion, ethnicity, occupation, and so forth. But it doesn't seem plausible to assume that husband's X *causes* wife's X, or vice versa. Instead, we draw curved arrows from spouse to spouse. The result is a system in which each generation forms a block (Figure 5 illustrates this).

When analyzing data, it is crucial to keep straight exactly where your variables are in the system. Notation and vocabulary can be helpful here. I find the following notation helpful:

(1) Designate each variable as X plus a number or number and letter (e.g., X2, X3c, X14).

(2) Numbers designate blocks, letters designate variables within a block. (Remember, a block may contain just one variable.)

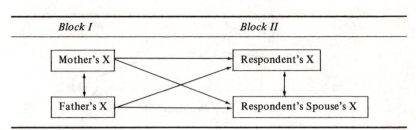

Figure 5   A Block System

For example, consider X2 or X3c. X2 is in the second block, preceded by either a single variable (which would be X1) or a block (X1a, X1b, etc.). X2 is the only variable in the second block (no letter). X3c is in a block of unordered variables (of which there are at least three, if the lettering convention is to start with a). There are two blocks (possibly two variables, possibly many more than two) earlier in the sequence than X3c.

It is also important to keep straight where a particular variable lies *relative to some pair* of Xs, say, for example, X8 and X14. Every other variable in a loop free system must be either

earlier than X8,

between X8 and X14,

later than X14, or

in the 8 or 14 block (if so, X8 and X14 would have letters as well as numbers).

If we designate the earlier member of the pair (e.g., X8) the *independent variable* and the later member (e.g., X14) the *dependent variable*, the following terminology applies:

(1) Variables preceding the independent variable are *prior variables*.

(2) Variables located between the independent and dependent variables are *intervening variables*.

(3) Variables coming after the dependent variable are *consequent variables*.

(4) Variables in the same blocks as the independent and dependent variables have no special name (and cause enormous trouble, as

we shall see later). Let's call them *parallel* variables, so we don't forget them.

(5) Xi and Xj mean *any arbitrarily chosen independent and dependent variables*.

Figure 6 illustrates this.

Prior ⟶ Independent ⟶ Intervening ⟶ Dependent ⟶ Consequent

Figure 6   Standard Nomenclature for Relative Position of Variables

Some examples from Figure 2:

In section a, for educational attainment and earnings, parental status is *prior*, occupational prestige is *intervening*. For educational attainment and occupational prestige, parental status is *prior*, earnings is *consequent*.

In section b, education and conformism are *intervening* variables for generation and tolerance.

In section c, for party identification and voting, social class and ethnic background are *prior*, and there is *no intervening variable*.

Bear in mind that these useful concepts—prior, intervening, and consequent—are doubly relative. They are relative to the model at hand. Just because you didn't put any variables between the independent and dependent variables in your model, you can't assume there aren't any in the real world. They are also relative to the independent and dependent variables you are talking about at the moment. Which variables are prior, intervening, or consequent depends entirely on which pair you selected for independent or dependent. Table 1 summarizes the possibilities in a four-variable, ordered system.

Econometrics applies similar concepts to entire systems. By definition, in an ordered or block recursive system there are no one-way arrows running into the first block. (If the block has two or more variables, one connects them with double-headed arrows.) Variables in block 1 are called exogenous, later variables are called endogenous. The exogenous variables are all priors, whose values are simply given and not analyzed;

TABLE 1
Nomenclature for Relative Order in a Four-Variable System

X	Y	Prior		Intervening		Consequent	
X1	X2	–		–		X3	X4
X1	X3	–		X2			X4
X1	X4	–		X2	X3	–	
X2	X3	X1		–		X4	
X2	X4	X1		X3		–	
X3	X4	X1	X2	–		–	

the endogenous variables are the dependent variables. In a sense, statistical analysis boils down to finding out whether the exogenous variables in the model influence the exogenous variables directly or via those endogenous variables that intervene.

EFFECTS: DIRECT VERSUS INDIRECT, CAUSAL VERSUS SPURIOUS

Once you have stated the assumed causal direction for each pair of variables and worked out the block structure of the system (the way to do this is to draw and redraw arrow diagrams until the blocks are arranged from left to right on the page and all one-way arrows are aimed to the right side of the page), you have *specified the system.* Your completed arrow diagram (often called a "path diagram" or "flow graph") is very much like the list of initial assumptions (axioms) in traditional logic. You say to yourself, "Given a system with this many variables arranged in this causal structure, what would happen if . . . "

What would happen to *what?* The main "whats" are *levels* (means) of particular variables and the *effects* of earlier variables on later ones. Thus, we use arrow diagrams to reason out the ways causal phenomena earlier in the system influence the levels and effects down stream. Levels are straightforward: We are almost always talking about means or percentages; for example, in section c of Figure 2 one might ask, "What would happen to the *proportion of Republicans* (level) if the social class composition of the electorate changed and class differences in Party Identification became stronger?"

Effects among variables are more complicated. They involve two distinctions: (1) direct versus indirect causal effects and (2) causal versus "spurious" effects. Let us start with direct and indirect causal effects.

Figure 7 shows a hypothetical four-variable system, with what look like extension cords running into each variable. This is done to point up

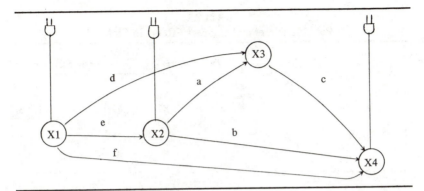

Figure 7   Hypothetical Four-Variable System

the differences between changes coming from outside the system (when we plug in one of the cords) and changes produced by variables in the system.

Assuming that all effects are positive (when X goes up, Y goes up; when X goes down, Y goes down), let us walk through a scenario beginning when something outside the system operates to raise (lower) the level of X2 (i.e., when its cord is plugged in):

(a) the level of X3 goes up (down);
(b) the level of X4 goes up (down).

These are the *direct* or *one-step* effects, a and b. They follow from the definition of one-way arrows. But that's not all.

The arrow from X3 to X4 says X3 has a direct effect on X4: When X3 goes up or down, X4 goes up or down. Now, going back to X2, if its level changes, the level of X3 will change, and if X3 changes, the level of X4 will change. Thus, in addition to X2's direct effect on X4 (arrow b), it has an indirect effect because it changes a variable that changes X4. This is called a *two-step* or *indirect* effect on a dependent variable.

The metaphor of ripples on a pond gives the flavor. In an ordered system when an earlier variable changes, it produces direct effects on all other variables "one arrowhead away" downstream, two-step indirect effects on all variables on which *they* have direct effects, three-step indirect effects on variables dependent on them, and so on. (This is not to say that these wide ripples are very powerful. Like the ripples in ponds, they tend to dampen quickly.)

TABLE 2
Possible Direct and Indirect Effects in Figure 7

X	Y	Direct	Two-Step via			Three-Step via			
X1	X2	e							
X1	X3	d	e	a	X2				
X1	X4	f	e	b	X2	e	a	c	X2, X3
			d	c	X3				
X2	X3	a							
X2	X4	b	a	c	X3				
X3	X4	c							

Note that a prior variable may have more than one effect on a particular dependent variable. In Figure 7, for example, X1 has the following effects on X4: a direct effect (f) two two-step indirect effects (e to b, d to c) and one three-step indirect effect (e to a to c).

Putting exactly the same idea in a slightly different fashion: When X changes it can have a direct effect on Y and also as many indirect effects as there are separate paths from X to Y via intervening variables. Consider, for example, Figure 7. Table 2 lists all the possible direct and indirect effects.

Indirect effects are not "phony." They are real, albeit complex, parts of the causal process. Tracing out direct and indirect effects is one of data analysis's important contributions to causal understanding. In actual research we never see these causal flows. We see their reflections in correlations (associations) among variables. It is like exploring the desert in the dry season and inferring where the streams flowed during the rainy season.

All other things equal, a direct causal flow from Xi to Xj should produce a cross-sectional correlation between them. If increases in Xi produce increases in Xj, at any given moment cases higher on Xi will tend to be higher on Xj, provided the research was carried out before the effect wears off and provided appropriate extraneous variables have been controlled.

The problem is not whether causal effects produce correlations, but whether correlations *imply* causal effects. We are all familiar with the slogan "correlation doesn't prove causation," but like most such aphorisms it is less clear than it seems. It does not mean causation can never be inferred from correlation. Thousands of well-trained, conservative data analysts make such inferences daily. In order to see what it does mean, we need a new concept, "slope coefficient." A slope coefficient is a number that tells us how much a dependent variable increases per unit increase in the independent variable. (The classic example is a b or beta in regression analysis, but we are not talking about any specific coefficient here.) For example, assume it is really true that each additional hour of study increases one's score on the final exam by one and one half points (on the average). If so, the slope for exam scores is 1.5 when the units are exam points and hours. Similarly, one might have slopes for the effects of TV advertising on sales volume, the effect of years of schooling on occupational prestige, the effect of group size on conformity, and so forth. (Nonlinear slopes make the calculations more complicated, but don't change any of the ideas here.)

In cross-sectional research we obtain scores on variables and examine their statistical relations; for example, calculate the correlation between exam scores and reported hours of study. Common sense suggests the cross-sectional slope from these calculations is a good estimate of the causal effect. If students one hour apart in study average 1.5 points apart in exam scores, it certainly looks as if an increase or decrease in hours of study would move one's grades about 1.5 points per hour.

But this doesn't have to be correct. It could be that the true slope is 0.5 or 2.8 or even 0.0 or -2.6. If so—if the cross-sectional slope is seriously different from the real slope—we say our coefficient is *spurious*. That is, *a correlation is spurious to the extent the cross-sectional slope differs from the true causal effect.*

What makes correlations spurious? Some obvious candidates are sampling bias, random sampling variation, invalid or unreliable measurements, and calculation errors. But spurious correlations or spurious components of a correlation can occur when the sampling, measurement, and calculations are impeccable. Indeed, spuriousity is almost inevitable in multivariate systems. Why? Because of causal order.

We are already familiar with the principle for the case of two variables. If, for example, we draw an arrow from X_i to X_j and the data give a slope of, say, 1.5, the 1.5 may be a good estimate of the effect of X_i on X_j, but it is totally spurious as an estimate of the effect of X_j on X_i. When we draw a one-way arrow from X_i to X_j, we believe the true reverse slope is zero. Consequently, mistakes about arrow directions are a source of spurious correlations. In addition to measurement problems, misspecification of causal directions can produce spuriousity.

But even when measurement is accurate and specification is correct, spuriousity can be generated by variables prior to the independent and

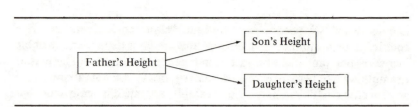

Figure 8

dependent variables. In fact, in social research the phrase "spurious correlation" is usually limited to this case of association produced by prior variables. Consider, for example, the heights of fathers, sons, and daughters, as displayed in Figure 8. I have drawn arrows from father to son and father to daughter because children's heights tend to line up with the heights of their parents. But I didn't draw anything between sons and daughters to emphasize the absence of any causal effect: Siblings' heights do not exert any influence on each other.

If we were to collect data on these three variables, we would find correlations between fathers' and offspring's heights. These reflect causal flows. We will also, however, find a cross-sectional statistical association between the heights of brothers and sisters. That slope is totally spurious. Nothing about a brother's height has a causal effect on his sister's height.

What actually does produce statistical association in the absence of any causal flow? It's quite simple, as shown in this example:

(1) Taller fathers produce taller sons (causal flow).
(2) Taller sons will be associated with taller fathers (spurious slope produced by 1).
(3) Taller fathers produce taller daughters (causal flow).
(4) Taller sons will be associated with taller daughters (they are associated with taller fathers, who produce taller daughters, producing a spurious association).

We can think of the substructures that produce spuriousity as "Vs" with a prior variable at the base of the V and arrows to the independent and dependent variable in question forming the two sides.

V structures are not limited to direct arrows. Prior variables way back in the system can produce spuriousity if they have a direct *or* indirect effect on both variables (the independent and dependent variables in question). The effect may be small and it may be offset by other factors, but it is always there and can be detected by statistical analyses to be explained later.

It is important to keep straight exactly what we mean by the word "spurious." We do not mean "imaginary." It is a true, scientifically verifiable fact that the average height of the brothers of tall sisters is greater than the height of brothers of shorter females. For purposes of *prediction* spurious associations can be invaluable. You could probably pick your college roommate's siblings out of a crowd without having met them. What is spurious in a spurious correlation is your estimate of the causal impact of manipulating the independent variable. In a sense, spuriousity is forecasting error. If we start a nutritional program for children in an underdeveloped area, we might forecast increased height for their unborn children, but it would be ridiculous to expect any changes in height for siblings not in the program. It is equally important to remember that spuriousity is a matter of degree. (That's why I use the awkward word spuriousity instead of talking about "spurious correlations.") Few correlations are totally spurious and few lack any influence from prior variables.

> *Rule 3:* If a prior variable has a causal path to the independent variable and a causal path to the dependent variable, it will contribute a statistical association between them that is causally spurious.

SIGNS AND THE SIGN RULE

Every variable is assigned plus and minus ends or poles. Usually they are obvious: For fertility, + means lots of children, – means zero; for education, + means many years, – means no years; for income, + means lots of money, – means red ink. Often, however, signing is arbitrary. Who is to say whether male or female should be +; who is to say that Republican is + and Democratic – ? Occasionally we reverse natural signs: When studying poverty we might wish to reverse the polarities for income, so that high poverty means low income.

With two signed variables their *relationship* has a sign (unless it is u-shaped). A *positive* relationship means as X goes up Y goes up, a *negative* relationship means as X goes up Y goes down.

It is useful to indicate the sign of a relationship when drawing the arrows. There is no standard convention, but I suggest:

$(X_i) - - \rightarrow (X_j)$ = negative

$(X_i) \longrightarrow (X_j)$ = positive

When one reverses polarities, one reverses the sign of the relationship. For example:

$(\text{education}) \xrightarrow{+} (\text{income})$ = the greater the education the greater the income

$(\text{ignorance}) - \overset{-}{-} \rightarrow (\text{income})$ = the greater the ignorance the less the income

$(\text{education}) - \overset{-}{-} \rightarrow (\text{poverty})$ = the greater the education the less the poverty

$(\text{ignorance}) \xrightarrow{+} (\text{poverty})$ = the greater the ignorance the greater the poverty

More formally:

Rule 4: Reversing poles for one variable reverses the signs of each of its relationships. Reversing polarities for both variables leaves the sign of their relationship unchanged.

In multivariate systems reversing polarities can change the physical appearance of the system considerably. Thus, it would not be obvious to the untutored eye that in Figure 9 systems a1 and a2 are really "the same" as are systems b1 and b3.

Polarity is a rhetorical problem, not a scientific or mathematical one. The goal is to assign polarities that help a reader understand his or her findings and to draw the arrow diagrams using whatever symbols and labels keep things clear. Generally speaking, things will be clearer if you assign polarities to maximize the number of positive arrows. More on this when we get to Rule 5.

Paths (routes following arrows) also have signs.

	Path Sign

I $(X1)\xrightarrow{+}(X2)\xrightarrow{+}(X3)\xrightarrow{+}(X4)$ +

II $(X1)\xrightarrow{+}(X2)\xrightarrow{-}(X3)\xrightarrow{-}(X4)$ +

III $(X1)\xrightarrow{+}(X2)\xrightarrow{-}(X3)\xrightarrow{+}(X4)$ −

IV $(X1)\xrightarrow{-}(X2)\xrightarrow{-}(X3)\xrightarrow{-}(X4)$ −

In Case I, an all-positive path, when X1 goes up, X2 goes up; when X2 goes up, X3 goes up; and when X3 goes up, X4 goes up. When X1 goes down it is the opposite. When X1 changes, it sets off a causal chain that eventually moves X4 the same way X1 shifted.

Case II contains negative arrows, but the final effect has the same sign as Case I. When X1 goes up, X2 goes up, which makes X3 go down; when X3 goes down, X4 goes up so after the dust has settled X4 moves in the same direction as X1.

Case III is a negative path: when X1 goes up, X2 goes up; when X2 goes up, X3 goes down; when X3 goes down, X4 goes down—so after the dust has settled, X4 moves in the opposite direction of changes in X1.

Case IV is also negative. You can work out the steps on your own to see why.

But you do not have to work out the sign of each path by reasoning out the steps. Instead, you apply the "sign rule."

Rule 5: The sign of a path is given by multiplying the sign of its arrows. A path of nonzero arrows will be positive unless it contains an odd number of negative arrows.

For example:

$(X1)\xrightarrow{-}(X2)\xrightarrow{+}(X3)\xrightarrow{-}(X4)\xrightarrow{+}(X5)\xrightarrow{+}(X6)$

Even though the path has six variables, five arrows, and both positive and negative relationships, a glance is sufficient to tell us the effect of X1 on X6 is positive, because the path contains an even number (two) of negative arrows.

The sign rule has some valuable corollaries:

(1) A path containing a zero arrow anywhere has a value of zero.

(2) Inserting any number of positive links in a causal chain has no effect on its sign.

(3) Inserting a single negative link anywhere reverses the sign of a chain.

V structures also have signs. In the simplest case, a three-variable system (prior, independent, and dependent) in which both sides of the V are direct, the sign of the spurious component is given by multiplying the signs of the two sides of the V. Consider the family height example: The sign for father and son is +, the sign for father and daughter is +, + times + = +, so father's height contributes a positive component to the brother-sister association. (An easy rule of thumb: If the prior variable has *same* sign effects on independent and dependent, it will have a positive effect on the correlation; if the prior's effects have *opposite* signs for independent and dependent, the spurious contribution will be negative.) When the V is more complex, special rules apply (they are explained later), but the general notion still holds—if a prior moves both in the same direction, it makes their correlation more positive (less negative); if it moves them in opposite directions, it makes their correlation more negative (less positive). The spurious component may be just a part of the total association, and it is possible other factors will push the opposite way. Thus, a prior variable may contribute a positive component to a correlation even though the total cross-sectional association ends up negative.

The notion of sign can be extended to systems as a whole. The main theme of the systems approach is that the total relationship between a pair of variables can be divided into (1) a direct effect, (2) one or more indirect paths, and (3) spurious components produced by paths from prior variables. How you put all of them together depends on the particular statistical scheme (percentages, raw regression coefficients, standardized regression coefficients), but the common theme is adding up causal components, which do not necessarily have the same signs. Figure 9 illustrates.

System a at the top and left of Figure 9 shows X1 and X4 connected by two intervening variables, X2 and X3. The system has both positive

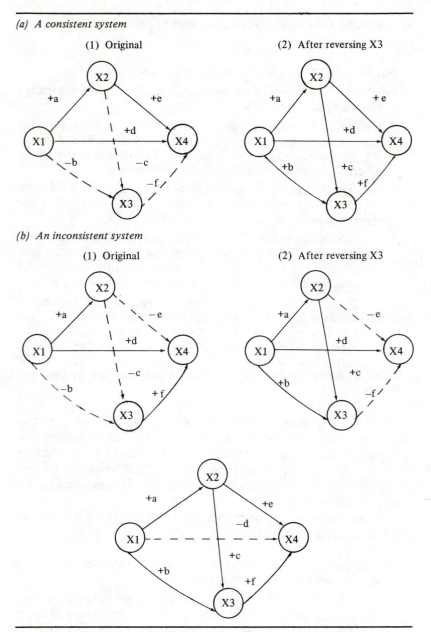

Figure 9   Consistent (Reinforcing) and Inconsistent (Suppressor) Systems

and negative arrows and positive and negative paths. Let's look at each pair.

For X1 and X2 there is a single *positive* arrow, +a.

For X1 and X3 there is a *negative* direct arrow, –b, and a *negative* two-step path via X2, +a, –c.

For X2 and X3 there is a *negative* direct arrow, –c, and a spurious contribution from X1. Since an increase in X raises X2 and lowers X3, the spurious effect will be negative. X1 will tend to contribute a *negative* component to the X2 X3 relationship.

For X1 and X4 there is a *positive* arrow, +d, a *positive* two-step path via X2, +a, +e, a *positive* two-step path via X3, –b, –f, and a *positive* three-step path via X2 and X3, +a, –c, –f.

For X2 and X4 there is a *positive* arrow, +e, a *positive* two-step path via X3, –c, –f, and a spurious contribution from X. We have seen that the effect of X1 and X2 is positive and both effects of X1 on X4 are positive. Therefore, the spurious component will be *positive*.

For X3 and X4 there is a *negative* arrow, –f, and a spurious contribution from X2. Since X2 has opposite effects on X3 and X4 (–c and +e) it will be *negative*. There also is a spurious contribution from X1. Since X1's paths to X3 are both negative and its paths to X4 are both positive, the spurious component will be *negative* because X1 will move X3 and X4 in opposite directions.

We see how complex and rich even a small system can be, but this recital also had a theme: For each pair of variables, all the components affecting the relationship have the same sign—each causal mechanism pushes the relationship in the same direction. Such systems are called *consistent* (no signs disagree) or *reinforcers* (the causal mechanisms reinforce each other).

For contrast, consider system 9b. The relations among X1, X2, and X3 are unchanged, but for X4:

For X1 and X4 the direct effect is *positive*, +d, and the indirect effects are all *negative* (+a, e) (–b, +f) (+a, –c, +f).

For X2 and X4 the direct effect is *negative*, –e, the indirect effect via X3 is *negative* (–c, +f), and the spurious contribution of X1 is *ambiguous*: X1 has a positive effect on X2, but its effect on X4 is both positive (+d) and negative (–b, +f).

For X3 and X4 the direct effect is *positive*, +f, the spurious component coming from X2 is *positive* (–e and –c), and the spurious component coming from X1 is *ambiguous*. X1 has a consistently negative effect on X3 but its effects on X4 are both positive (+d) and negative (+a, –e).

Such systems are called *inconsistent* (some components in a relationship have opposite signs) or *suppressors* (effects working in opposite directions reduce the total size of the relationship, i.e., they "suppress" each other).

Reinforcer and suppressor effects are important substantively and technically. Substantively, reinforcer systems have a "them as has gets" flavor. Social class correlations between parents and children tend to have this character: High parental status not only has a direct positive effect on children's achievement, it also leads to intervening variables, especially educational attainment, that reinforce the effect. Conversely, suppressor systems illustrate the sociological concepts of "unanticipated consequences," in which change in X has a certain influence on Y, but X also sets off other causal chains that tend to undo or dampen the effect. An example from voting research: Educational attainment tends to move one toward a liberal position on social issues (education and liberalism are +) but it also leads to increased income (education and income are +), and increased income tends to make one less liberal (income and liberal are –). Thus, education is linked to liberalism by a + direct path and a negative (+ times – = –) two-step path. Education, income, and liberalism form an inconsistent system. On the technical side, in a reinforcer system the direct effect of Xi on Xj is always the same or smaller than the total effect; in a suppressor system, the direct effect may be larger than the total (sum of all effects). More on this later.

A simple test tells whether a system is consistent. One reverses polarities for the variable with the largest number of negative signs following Rule 4, then repeats the process as long as possible. If all the negative signs go away, the system is consistent. In system a of Figure 9, after we reverse poles for X3, all arrows are positive. In system b, however, we reverse X3, which brings the negative arrows down from three to two. Then we reverse X4. This leaves us with one negative arrow (–d) but there are no further changes that would decrease the number of arrows.

> *Rule 6:* A system is inconsistent if at least one pair of variables has both positive and negative signs among its direct, indirect, and spurious effects. Otherwise, it is consistent. If a system is consistent, all negative arrows can be eliminated by reversing polarities.

In sum, variables have + and – poles and relationships have + and – signs. Polarities are often arbitrary, but it is still important to keep them straight and to choose them so as to keep things clear. Because paths are constructed from relationships, they have signs: Whether or not the ultimate influence of Xi on Xj is positive or negative depends on whether or not the path connecting them has an odd number of negative links. In a system each relationship may be affected by direct links, longer paths, and spurious contributions from prior variables. When the components are both positive and negative, the system is inconsistent or a suppressor. Otherwise, it is consistent or reinforcing. In a reinforcing system one may make all nonzero links positive by reversing polarities.

2. USING THE LOGIC

The working parts—variables, assumptions about one-way causal flows, systems with order or loops, and statistical effects, which may be direct, indirect, or causally spurious, positive, negative, consistent, or inconsistent—have been explained. Now we consider how the research worker actually uses these ideas.

In a sense, data analysis consists of estimating slope coefficients with and without particular variables "controlled." Imagination, scholarship, and good luck are necessary to choose the most telling variables, but once this is done, statistical analysis boils down to making a series of "runs" in which one examines relationships (slopes) with this, that, and the other variable controlled or decontrolled.

This is a bit like saying all there is to painting is choosing colors from a palette and filling the canvas with them. Yet it does provide a theme for what otherwise would seem a totally disorganized fishing expedition. Most questions about data analysis boil down to, "What are you controlling? Why these controls? What will that tell you?"

How to control is a technical statistical matter, but the underlying reasoning can be seen with simple arrow diagrams. Consider a classical randomized experiment. Suppose, for example, we wish to study the effects of classroom size on learning. We could (1) assign students to classes of various sizes *randomly*, for example, by coin flips, (2) offer

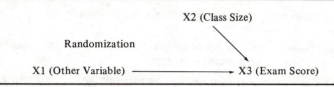

Figure 10   Hypothetical Experiment

similar instruction in each class, (3) give all the students the same final exam, and (4) compare the exam scores of the classes. If there are nonrandom differences among the classes in their exam scores, we will infer class size influences learning. This design can be expressed in terms of three variables: X2 = classroom size; X3 = exam score; X1 = other variable. Figure 10 shows the system.

The "experimental effect" may be viewed as a cross-sectional correlation between X2 and X3. If nonzero, is it causal? Or is it contaminated by "spuriousity?" It is causal. Why am I so sure? Well, by definition, spuriousity occurs when a prior variable, such as X1, influences X2 and X3. But when we assigned students randomly, we severed any possible connections between X1 and X2, so there is no V-structure. If there is no V-structure, there is no spurious component in the correlation. The intellectual beauty of randomized design is this: We do not have to know the names of any of the prior valuables that need control. Randomly constituted classes will show only random differences (no X1 X2 correlation) for *any* prior variable whatsoever.

Now let's consider a nonexperimental, cross-sectional design in which we gather "real world" data on class size and test scores (i.e., one in which the students were assigned to classes however real students are assigned to real classes). Oh dear! There is no end to the possible X1 variables that could produce V-structures. Smarter students might prefer smaller classes, pull strings to get assigned there, and do better on the exams; trouble-makers might be assigned to smaller classes so teachers can keep an eye on them, and trouble-makers might have lower exam scores; students from high-status backgrounds might be better able to afford elite, private schools with smaller classes, and high-status students might score better, and so forth and so on.

The all-purpose spuriousity insurance of randomization is no longer available, but if we can measure likely prior variables, we can control for them by statistical adjustments. Such controls are just as effective as random assignments—the problem is we can never know about the effects of variables we didn't measure.

Statistical control can be achieved in several ways:

In regression analysis control is achieved by "residualization" (explained in most statistics texts).

In tabular analysis it is done by "replication within control categories." (E.g., to control for sex, one repeats the analysis separately among men and among women. Within one sex, sex *differences* cannot be influencing the result.)

In demography one frequently standardizes or reweights the data to eliminate any X1 X2 differences (e.g., controlling for sex by weighting the number of male and female cases so each level of X2 has the same sex ratio).

No matter how it is done, every form of control amounts to some trick that gets rid of an X1 X2 correlation (sometimes X1 X3 also) so the cross-sectional slope for X2 and X3 is not contaminated by X1's spurious effects. Control obviously is a good thing and the rule of thumb is, the more elaborate the controls, the better the research. But you don't just control everything in sight. Rather, the logic of causal order allows you to target your controls toward specific questions.

The most common goal is to estimate a direct effect. This is explained in the next section. But since a relationship usually comprises a bundle of direct, indirect, and spurious parts, one almost always wishes to go beyond direct effects and divide the relationship into its component parts, analysis in its literal sense. Several strategies—ranging from the simplicity of "Lazarsfeldian elaboration" to the rococo of path analysis—are explained in the following section.

Estimating Direct Effects

The technical details of calculating direct effects (slopes) depend on the statistic (r, phi, gamma, q, b, beta, d, etc.) but the logic of causal order tells *what* to control regardless of the calculation.

Consider, for example, the relationship between X2 and X4 in system a of Figure 9, coefficient e. We wish to end up with a number, such as e = .345 or e = .000, or e = −16.217. An "obvious" way to estimate e would be to make repeated observations of X2 and X4 (e.g., tiptoe out every morning for six months and observe them). If X2 scores fluctuate, you could then work out the increase or decrease in X4 per unit change in X2.

The obvious way is, of course, wrong. Why? Two reasons: First, it ignores X3. When X2 changes, it sets off changes in X3, and these trigger changes in X4. The raw fluctuations include not only e, but the positive effects of the indirect path –c, –f. Second, there is X1, the prior variable. It may have been oscillating wildly all during the observation period, producing spurious coordination in the movements of X2 and X4.

If we could prevent X1 from changing and prevent X3 from changing, then any coordination in X2 and X4 must be due to the arrow d (or variables outside the system that we neglected in our specifications; this problem is discussed in the last section).

When we control a variable, we often say that it is partialled out and hence, the following standard vocabulary:

> *Bivariate* relationship = the relationship between Xi and Xj with no variables controlled.

> *Partial* relationship = the relationship between Xi and Xj with one or more variables controlled.

What variables shall we control? The answer is easy: As priors and intervening variables can influence the relationship, they must be controlled.

By definition, consequent variables, those coming after the dependent variable in the causal sequence, cannot influence Xi or Xj directly or indirectly. They should never be controlled. Indeed, if one controls on a consequent variable, queer and confusing things can happen. So it boils down to a simple rule:

> *Rule 7:* When estimating the effect of Xi on Xj, control all prior and intervening variables; that is, control all variables not consequent to Xj.

Following Rule 7 one may estimate the arrows in an ordered system by working from beginning to end, adding controls as shown in Table 3. Each row in Table 3 tells us what to control when estimating the direct effect for a particular pair. Thus, the fifth line down tells us to control the prior variable X1 and the intervening variable X3 when estimating the direct effect of X2 on X4; the bottom line tells us to control the three prior variables, X1, X2, and X3, when estimating the direct effect of X4 on X5. Note that when X and Y are the first two variables in the sequence, nothing is controlled because none of the variables in the system is intervening or prior for X1 and X2.

TABLE 3
Controls in an Ordered Five-Variable System

1	2	3	4	5
(X1)	(X2)			
(X1)	i	(X3)		
p	(X2)	(X3)		
(X1)	i	i	(X4)	
p	(X2)	i	(X4)	
p	p	(X3)	(X4)	
(X1)	i	i	i	(X5)
p	(X2)	i	i	(X5)
p	p	(X3)	i	(X5)
p	p	p	(X4)	(X5)

NOTE: i = intervening control; p = prior control.

Some statistical routines, in particular "multiple regression," do not ask you to distinguish between control and independent variables. They ask you to choose a dependent variable and a set of prior variables. Then for each prior variable the computer calculates its net (direct) effect controlling for all the other priors. Thus, with dependent variable E and prior variables A, B, C, and D, the computer will automatically give you the effect of A on E, controlling for B, C, and D; of B on E, controlling for A, C, and D; the effect of C on E, controlling for A, B, and D; and the effect of D on E, controlling for A, B, and C. Fine! That makes life simple: Once you have chosen a dependent variable, all you need do is enter *everything before it* into the regression equation. The computer will then automatically give you a complete array of net effects, each with its proper controls. Rule 7a puts it succinctly:

> *Rule 7a:* In multiple regression, regress each variable on all its predecessors.

If, Heaven forbid, one were interested in the arrow from X38 to X72 in a 100 variable system, one would simply tell the computer to create a regression equation in which the dependent variable is X72 and the predictors are X1 through X71. The coefficient for X38 is the value of the arrow for X38 and X72 with X1 through X37 and X39 through X71 controlled.

Strategies for Analysis

Estimation of direct effects is not the be all and end all of data analysis. You can be seriously misled if you take them at face value.

Think of them as the wires in an electronic gadget or the bricks in a building: crucial components, but one can't tell how the gadget or building functions until one sees how the parts fit together and what they do. Thus, nontrivial data analysis goes beyond laying out the causal diagram (specification) and ascertaining the coefficients for each arrow (estimation) to causal analyses that illuminate how the system works.

All analyses need not be causal.

In prediction one seeks the best combination of Xs for estimating values of some dependent variables (e.g., predicting freshman grades from high school grades, SAT scores, and family background or predicting presidential vote from unemployment rates, presidential popularity ratings, and the number of woolly caterpillars on the trees). Prediction is not easy—unlike woolly caterpillars, strong correlations do not grow on trees—but its logic is simple. One merely assembles promising Xs and then finds the most efficient combination of predictors.

In causal understanding one seeks insight into how the system works, not just the sizes of the relationships. For example:

—Are ethnic differences in party preference really due to social class?

—Are better educated people really more tolerant, or is the correlation spurious?

—What are the variables that explain why parents and children are similar in occupational prestige?

—Are sex differentials in earnings due to the greater seniority of male workers?

In each case the answer turns more on the structure of the system—the signs, paths, spurious components, intervening variables—than on the magnitude of the direct association.

Social scientists use several strategies for causal analysis. We will review three: Lazarsfeldian elaboration, Hauser and Alwin's Effect Analysis, and Sewall Wright's Path Analysis. The three-fold division is handy, but you should remember (1) all three use the same underlying principles of causal order logic and (2) they are mutually inclusive, not mutually exclusive; they differ mostly in how much detail you get.

ELABORATION AND EXPLANATION

The classic strategy for causal understanding was proposed by the late Paul F. Lazarsfeld, is called "elaboration," and centers on the notion of "explanation."

It goes like this: First, we observe a two variable (*bivariate*) association between X_i and X_j. Second, we advance the hypothesis that a *test variable*, X_t, accounts for correlation. Third, we *elaborate* the analysis by introducing X_t into the calculation. Fourth, we examine the correlation between X_i and X_j after X_t has been controlled. If the partial association between X_i and X_j becomes zero, we say X_t *explains* the X_iX_j correlation.

Some examples—perhaps a bit overdrawn to make the logic clear:

> *Q: Why is there more delinquency among lower-status youth?*
> *A: Because of broken homes.*

If so, we will find

(1) a bivariate correlation between social class and delinquency;
(2) the partial correlation between class and delinquency becomes zero when we control for parental family composition.

> *Q: Why do European nations have lower birth rates than developing nations?*
> *A: Because of their aging populations.*

If so, we will find

(1) a bivariate correlation between region and birth rate;
(2) the partial correlation between region and birth rate becomes zero when we control for median age of the nation.

> *Q: Why do Blacks prefer the Democratic Party?*
> *A: Because of social class.*

If so, we will find

(1) a bivariate correlation between race and party ID;
(2) the partial correlation between race and party ID becomes zero when we control for social class.

> *Q: Why are Jews so liberal on political issues?*
> *A: Because of their higher educations and urban residences.*

If so, we will find

(1) a bivariate correlation between religion (Jewish versus other) and issue position;

(2) the partial correlation between religion and issue becomes zero when we control for education and size of place.

When they work, elaboration and explanation are powerful and elegant. They allow us to compress complicated matters into two numbers (the bivariate and partial relationship). They are intuitively persuasive ("now you see it, now you don't"). And, as the example of Judaism and issues illustrates, the idea can be extended to as many control variables as you wish.

The main drawback is that explanation is seldom perfect. Although it is not hard to find test variables that reduce a correlation, it is rare to drive a correlation to zero. When we do, it was usually a small correlation to begin with. If, as a fictitious example, the bivariate relationship between religion and issue position is +.25 and the partial, controlling for education and size of place is +.18, we are left with the rather limp conclusion, "education and size of place contribute to the correlation, but they do not completely explain it."

Thus, it is important to pick the best test variables. The sign rule (Rule 5) is a useful guide in finding test variables. Figure 11 shows how to apply it. Applying Rule 7, section a of Figure 11 says that X_i and X_t have a positive bivariate relationship; X_t and X_j have a positive relationship, controlling for X_i; the correlation between X_i and X_j is zero when X_t is controlled (no arrow).

What can we deduce about the bivariates involving the dependent variable, X_j? The X_tX_j bivariate will be positive and the same as the partial. Since there is no direct path from X_i to X_j, variable X_i contributes no spurious component to X_tX_j. The X_iX_j bivariate will be positive. The bivariate will be a combination of the indirect effect, which will be positive because both links are positive, and the direct, which is zero. In fact, the bivariate relationship for X_i and X_j will be exactly the same as the size of the two-step path.

Aha! Since the X_iX_j bivariate is positive and the X_iX_j partial is zero, X_t explains X_iX_j! (Note that when explaining this positive relationship, X_t has positive bivariates with X_i and X_j.)

Next is section c of Figure 11. It is exactly the same as section a except that the arrows are negative. As a result the X_iX_j bivariate will be

42

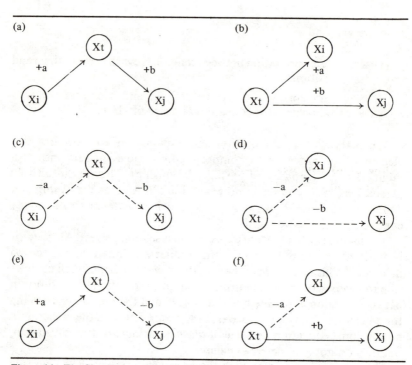

Figure 11   The Sign Rule and Promising Test Variables

positive (2 negatives are an even number). Xt's two negative bivariates explain a positive XiXj.

Third is section e. Here the test variable has a positive relationship with Xi, a negative relationship with Xj, and the XiXj bivariate that is explained will be negative, as the two-step path has one negative link.

Any forest among the trees? Sure.

When Xt explains XiXj, it does so by producing an indirect path or u structure with the same sign as the bivariate XiXj.

If both links, XtXi and XtXj, are positive XiXj will be positive.

If both links, XtXi and XtXj, are negative, XiXj will be positive.

If one link is positive the other link negative, XiXj will be negative.

When the XiXj direct effect is zero, the bivariates for Xt will be identical to their values in the three variable graph.

Hence:

> *Rule 8:* A test variable, Xt, explains XiXj when the XiXj bivariate is nonzero and the XiXj partial, controlling for Xt, is zero or trivially small. To explain a positive correlation, look for Xts where XtXi and XtXj have the same sign. To explain a negative correlation, look for Xts where XtXi and XtXj have opposite signs.

The three figures at the right side of Figure 11 have exactly the same signs and exactly the same conclusions as those on the left. The only difference is that their test variable is prior. The notion of explanation is indifferent to whether the test variable is prior or intervening—although it would be illogical to use a Xt that is consequent for Xj.

The rule is used every day in research to find promising test variables. Here is an example: Assume we find a positive correlation between region and attitudes such that southerners are more conservative. We ask why. Consider three possible test variables: sex, race, and education. Which shall we try? I say education but not sex or race:

> *Education:* Since southerners are a bit lower on schooling XtXi = –; since schooling makes one less conservative, XtXj is –; – * – = + and XiXj is also +.

This matches the second part of Rule 8.

> *Sex:* Since there is no relationship between sex and region (males and females are equally common in the South and North), XtXi is 0 and whatever XtXj might be, 0 * anything is zero, not +.

> *Race:* Assuming Black is +, there is a positive correlation between race and region so XtX1 is +; Blacks tend to be liberal, not conservative, so XtXj is –; + * – = –, not +.[2]

Of the three, educational attainment seems the best bet as an explainer. The results for race suggest it might be a suppressor (see the earlier discussion of consistent and inconsistent systems)—when we control for race the correlation between region and conservativism might well be stronger. Interesting indeed, not an explanation of the association.

You never know until you actually calculate the results, but mental experiments using the sign rule are probably the most common form of reasoning for the working data analyst. In particular, the example of sex illustrates an important corollary of the explanation rule: *Unless Xt is related to both Xi and Xj, it is a poor candidate for explainer.*

Thus, since race and sex are totally unrelated, it is never worth the trouble to introduce race as a test variable for a correlation between sex and Xj and equally fruitless to introduce sex as an explainer for a race correlation.

In sum, data analysis often centers on the question "Why are Xi and Xj correlated?" An operational answer, proposed by Paul Lazarsfeld, is that we know why if we can make the correlation appear (bivariate) or disappear (partial) by elaborating our analysis to include one or more test variables. If we can drive the partial to zero (well, almost zero) by introducing Xt, we say that Xt explains XiXj. Given the logic of causal systems, we have a rule for spotting promising test variables for the XtXi and XtXj bivariates—when XiXj is positive, look for matching signs; when XiXj is negative, look for opposite signs.

EFFECTS ANALYSIS

The two numbers in elaboration analysis are certainly concise, but they conceal scads of information. By calculating a third correlation— the relationship between Xi and Xj controlling for priors only—we can expand our information considerably. This approach is known as "effects analysis" or "the decomposition of effects." (The scheme is the work of many hands. The bellwether papers in chronological order are Finney [1972]; Alwin and Hauser [1975]; Lewis-Beck and Mohr [1976].) It does not contradict Lazarsfeldian elaboration in any way. Instead, it is a simple and powerful extension—an elaboration of the elaboration principles.

Consider, in Figure 12, the well-known system for looking at intergenerational occupational mobility (i.e., the correlation between the prestige of father's and son's jobs). I picked father's job prestige (social standing) as Xi and schooling as Xj. Thus, I defined my research problem as this: How does a father's job influence his son's schooling? (As the data came from high school graduates, the question is how father's job influences going to college.) Given this problem and the Sewell-Hauser specification of causal order, mother's and father's educations are prior variables. If they are related to father's job and to

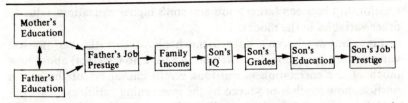

NOTE: Arrows for nonadjacent pairs removed for simplicity. Variables are in strict causal order, except for first two.

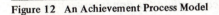

Figure 12 An Achievement Process Model

schooling, they will contribute spuriousity to the cross-sectional correlation. Family income, son's IQ, and son's high school grades are intervening variables. They define possible causal paths for the flow of influence from father's job to son's schooling.

Sewell and Hauser, in a classic study, collected data on these (and other) variables for a sample of 1,789 young men, graduated from Wisconsin high schools in 1957 and followed up in 1964. Effects analysis, like elaboration, is not tied to any particular statistical scheme. Sewell and Hauser analyze their data with standardized partial regression coefficients: numbers that range from .000 to +/– 1.00 that estimate slopes (change in the dependent variable per unit change in the independent) in the coinage of standard deviations. For example, a coefficient of +.30 says "a one standard deviation difference in the independent variable produces three-tenths of a standard deviation difference in the dependent."

The bivariate (nothing controlled) coefficient for X_i and X_j is +.290: the higher the prestige of the father's job, the more years of posthigh school education the young Wisconsin man completed.

When the priors (mother's and father's educations) and intervenors (income, IQ, and grades) are all controlled, the net coefficient is +.103. In Lazarsfeldian terms:

Unexplained (net)	+.103	36%
Explained (.290-.103)	+.187	64%
Total (bivariate)	+.290	100%

When we elaborate the analysis by introducing the five test variables, we can explain about two-thirds (64%) of the association. Most of the relationship between father's job and son's higher education is due to other variables in the model.

Fine, but we haven't learned much about how the various test variables are operating. In particular, we have no idea (yet) about how much of the correlation is spurious versus causal or, of the causal portion, how much is produced by the intervening variables.

One simple additional run will enable us to gain valuable detail. Simply run the correlation (or whatever statistic) between X_i and X_j, *controlling for all priors but not controlling for any intervenors.*

What will that tell you? If causal order has been correctly specified, the new coefficient will be the total causal effect of X_i on X_j. It will be causal because all priors have been controlled, it will be total because both direct effects and indirect effects via intervenors have been left in.

In the Sewell-Hauser data the causal coefficient = +.182. This is the standardized partial regression coefficient for father's job and son's education controlling for two variables, mother's and father's educations.

We now have three numbers, +.290 (bivariate), +.103 (net), and +.182 (causal). Table 4 shows us what to do with them. In Table 4, A, the total, is the bivariate correlation between X_i and X_j, their correlation (whatever statistic you might use) with nothing controlled. In our example it is +.290. B, the causal, is the correlation between X_i and X_j with prior variables only controlled. The correlation between father's and son's occupations controlling for parental schooling is +.182. C, the direct, is the correlation between X_i and X_j controlling for both prior and intervening variables. In our example this is +.103.

From these three numbers, we may calculate two more: D, the spurious portion of the correlation, is obtained by subtracting the causal from the total. In our example this is .290 – .182 = +.108. E, the indirect portion, is obtained by subtracting the direct from the causal, since any difference between them must be due to the presence or absence of the intervening variables. In our example this is .182 – .103 = +.079.

It is sometimes helpful to arrange the numbers like this:

$$
\text{causal} \,.182 \,(63\%) \begin{cases} .103 & (36\%) \\[6pt] .079 & (27\%) \end{cases}
$$

$$
\left. \begin{array}{l} \\ .108 \quad (37\%) \end{array} \right\} .187 \,(64\%)\ \text{explained}
$$

$$
\underline{\hphantom{.108}} \\ .290 \quad (100\%)
$$

TABLE 4
Effects Analysis

Effect	All Priors	All Intervenings	Sewell-Hauser Data
		Controlling	
(A) Total (bivariate)	no	no	+.290
(B) Causal	yes	no	+.182
(C) Direct (arrow est.)	yes	yes	+.103
(D) = A − B = spurious, due to priors			+.108
(E) = B − C = indirect, due to intervenors			+.079

From which we can spin a surprisingly detailed story:

The total effect of father's job on son's education is +.290. Of that, about two-thirds (.182 units or 63%) is causal. We would expect a unit change in father's job to produce a .182 change in son's schooling, even though the cross-sectional difference is .290.

A little less than half of the causal effect (.079 of .182 points or 43%) operates via the intervening variables: income, IQ, and grades. But 10 points (36% of the total, 57% of the causal) remain after the intervening variables have been controlled. Among sons matched on wealth, intelligence, and grades, those from higher occupational strata show higher educational attainments.

A third of the cross-sectional correlation is spurious. Parental schoolings operate to make the cross-sectional difference larger than the causal effect we would expect from differences in father's occupation alone.

Note the % here is the percentage of the relationship or association explained. It is not the percentage of the variance in the dependent variable explained. The latter, symbolized by "R square," is a very different matter.

Thus, the calculation of one additional relationship (a trivial task with any computerized statistical package) enables one to extend Lazarsfeldian elaboration to a profile of effects that describes the major causal components in the correlation between X_i and X_j.

> *Rule 9:* In addition to the X_iX_j bivariate (A) and the direct X_iX_j effect (C), calculate the causal effect (B) by controlling for prior variables only. Then find the spurious component (A-B) and the indirect portion due to intervening variables (B-C).

The three coefficients of effects analysis tell a surprisingly full story, but they do not tell the whole story. In the Sewell-Hauser data, for example, we still do not know *how* the intervening variables work—whether each of them mediates the effect of father's job on schooling or, perhaps, the linkage is entirely due to income (or IQ or grades). And we don't know a thing about the relative effects of the two parental educations.

Frequently (but not always) we wish to tease out the fine-grain detail of exactly how each variable and causal structure contributes to a particular relationship. Path analysis does exactly this.

FLOW GRAPHS AND PATH ANALYSIS

Again, let me stress that elaboration, effects analysis, and path analysis are *not* different techniques in the sense that surgery and medicine are different techniques. Rather, they are conventions about levels of detail, just as telescopes, field glasses, and microscopes are essentially similar gadgets. For textbook writing I have separated them because I think that is clearer. In practice, the data analyst uses all of them all the time and decides at the end how much detail to report.

Unlike elaboration and effects analysis, path analysis is limited to specific statistical techniques, in particular, raw and standardized multiple regression (see Heise, 1975: chap. 4), and weighted regression with proportions or percentage differences (see Davis, 1975; Taylor, 1983).

Although the principles of elaboration and effects analysis are valid for *any* data in which causal order is assumed, no matter what the statistics, for some statistical procedures path analysis simply doesn't work—if you make the calculations, you will get wrong answers. In particular, the currently fashionable log linear techniques for analyzing tables don't work this way. (In the abstract, the issue is whether the approach is part of the "general linear model." Whenever the data are analyzed so levels of variables are treated as dependent in linear equations, path-flow-graph principles apply.) In addition, it makes a difference whether you are decomposing intervening variable structures or prior variable structures.

To summarize, do path-flow-graph principles apply to . . .

Statistics	Prior Variables?	Intervening Variables?
Multiple Regression		
standardized coefficients	Yes	Yes
raw coefficients	No	Yes
Partial percentage differences	No	Yes
Log linear coefficients and odds ratios	No	No

To carry out path analyses you must know more about the details of these procedures than I can cover here but I will explain the principles as they follow directly from the logic of causal flows.

A path, you will remember, is a route from X_i to X_j following one-way arrows. Paths have signs: They may be positive, negative, or zero. They also have sizes or magnitudes, numbers that summarize the total impact on X_j of a unit change in X_i after it has rippled through the system. As a fictitious for instance, let's assume:

—a year's experience raises one's income $500;

—a dollar of income raises one's score on some measure of conservativism by .025 points;

—a point on the conservativism scale raises the percentage who vote Republican by .137 percentage points.

Now, let's assume some workers gain five years of experience. What will happen?

Their incomes will go up $2500 (5 × $500 = $2500).

A $2500 increase in income will raise their conservativism 62.5 points ($2500 × .025 = 62.5).

The 62.5 point increase in conservativism will raise their Republicanism 8.56 points (62.5 × .137 = 8.56).

Thus, a five-point gain in experience raises the Republican percentage 8.56 points; one year would produce a 1.71 shift (8.56/5 = 1.71); 20 years would make a 34.2 point increase (20 × 1.71 = 34.2). This story problem, of course, is a verbal version of a causal path, shown in Figure 13. Now, let's just multiply the three coefficients, a, b, and c: 500 × .025 × .137 = 1.7125.

All of which illustrates this principle: The value of a path (the change in Xj per change in Xi) is found by multiplying the coefficients of each arrow in the path. Regardless of the measurement units of the intervening variables, the result will come out in Xj units per one unit difference in Xi.

In real world systems variables are connected by more than one path, as shown in Figure 14.

Table 5 lists all the forward paths and their values in such a system. At first glance, the algebraic expressions in Table 5 do not seem interesting. But, after one gets used to them, they can be quite informative: With two intervenors (e.g., X1 to X4 or X2 to X5) each two-term path tells the independent effect of one intervenor, the three-term path gives their joint effect. Thus, for example, in an analysis of X1X4, if a*e is large and the other two terms small, you would conclude X2 is a more important intervenor than X3. It is also possible that both two step paths are small. If so, the system may be interpreted as a causal chain, like this:

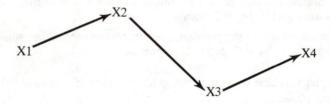

Such fine-grain detail is necessary when dealing with the slippery but politically potent notions of "vicious circle," "cycle of poverty," or "cumulative advantage." Consider the following argument:

Occupational and social status are to an important extent self-perpetuating. They are associated with many factors which make it difficult for individuals to modify their status. Position in the social structure is usually associated with a certain level of income, education, family structure, community reputation, and so forth. These become part of a vicious circle in which each factor acts on the other in such a way as to preserve the social structure in its present form.

a = $500	b = .025	c = .137

| Years of Experience | $\longrightarrow$ | Dollars of Income | $\longrightarrow$ | Scores on Conservatism | $\longrightarrow$ | Percentage Republican |

Figure 13   Hypothetical Causal Path

In their classic study of mobility, Peter Blau and O. D. Duncan (1967) note such pseudo-precise prose blurs the difference between two possible structures.

In either model the intervening variables explain the correlation between father's and son's educations (i.e., why the system is self-perpetuating). Effects analysis cannot distinguish between them. But the system in section a of Figure 15 is *cumulative*. Father's education has three separate paths to son's education and they add up (cumulate) to the bivariate. And the system in section b is *noncumulative*. All the intervening variables lie on a single path. There is no link from X to Y involving one of them that does not involve the others. Each plays a crucial part, but the parts do not cumulate. In sum, Xi has cumulative effects on Xj to the extent Xi and Xj are linked by multiple paths with distinct arrows.

For the applied sociologist, the distinction between cumulative and noncumulative structures can be crucial. In section a one would have to cut three different links (fund three separate federal agencies) to eliminate self-perpetuation. In section b you could get the same result by snipping any one of the links, perhaps the cheapest one, or the one that would produce the smallest political backlash.

With three or more intervenors linkages can be elaborate: for example, the eight paths linking X1 and X5 in Figure 14 and Table 5. As in any simple algebraic problem, the letters can be collected and arranged in a variety of ways. One way is to find the paths that do and do not operate through a particular intervenor. Thus, for X1X5 in Table 5, we see the example in Table 6.

Each row in Table 6 is a different rearrangement of the paths from X1 to X5. Each is divided into three portions: (I) the path or paths from XI to the intervening variable, (II) the path or paths from the intervenor to X5, and (III) all other paths from X1 to X5 not involving the intervenor in question. If you multiply the I terms by the II terms in a given line, you get the sum of the path effects that involve that intervenor. The bigger the sum, the more important the intervenor. (An example is coming up soon.)

52

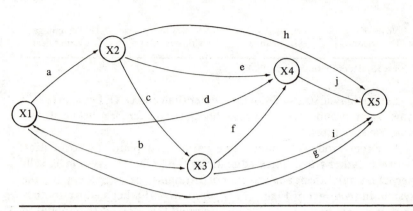

Figure 14 A Five-Variable Ordered System

Although the relative sizes of the various paths illuminate how causal flows actually work, their absolute values follow a famous principle:

> *Rule 10:* In a linear system the total causal effect of Xi on Xj is the sum of the values of all the paths from Xi to Xj.

The rule says if we specify the system correctly, obtain valid estimates of the arrow coefficients, multiply coefficients to find the value of each path, and sum the path values, the grand total will be the slope for the causal effect of Xi on Xj.

TABLE 5
Causal Paths in a Five-Variable System

Xi	to	Xj	Paths
1		2	a
1		3	b + a*c
2		3	c
1		4	d + a*e + b*f + a*c*f
2		4	e + c*f
3		4	f
1		5	g + a*h + b*i + d*j + a*c*i + a*e*j + b*f*j + a*c*f*i
2		5	h + e*j + c*i + c*f*j
3		5	i + f*j
4		5	j

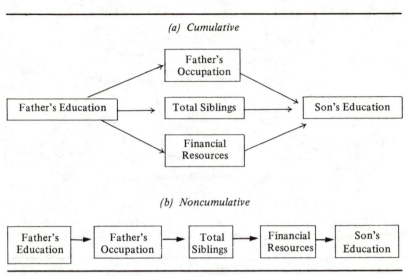

(a) Cumulative

(b) Noncumulative

Figure 15   Cumulative and Noncumulative Effects

Actually, we don't need the rule to find the causal effect. Rule 9 gave us a much simpler way. Instead, we use it backwards: Given the causal effect, Rule 10 guarantees that we can dissect it exactly into its component paths, data analysis in its most literal sense.

The effect of father's job prestige on son's schooling in the Sewell-Hauser data is a nice example. Figure 16 gives the coefficients, standardized partial regression coefficients. Mother's and father's educations were controlled in all estimates—their contribution will be scrutinized in the next section.

Path diagrams (arrow charts like Figure 16 with standardized partial regression coefficients) are endemic in professional social science journals. Although they are about the only art work one sees in publications such as *The American Sociological Review*, they are

TABLE 6
Alternate Decompositions of Paths from X1 to X5 in Table 5

Intervenor	*(I)* X1 to Intervenor	*	*(II)* Intervenor to X5	+	*Not Via Intervenor*
X2	((a)	*	(h + c*i + e*j + c*f*j)) +		(b*i + d*j + b*f*j)
X3	((b + a*c)	*	(i + f*j))	+	(a*h + d*j + a*e*j)
X4	(d + a*e + b*f + a*c*f)	*	((j))	+	(a*h + b*i + a*c*i)

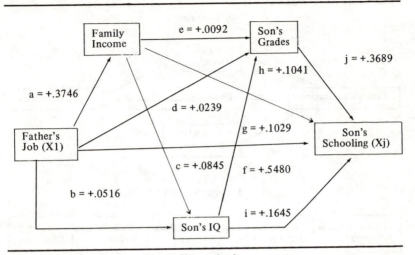

Figure 16   Path Coefficients (Sewell-Hauser data)

difficult to grasp (especially when the artist makes no attempt to arrange the variables in clear-cut causal order). The main problem is, as usually drawn, itty bitty coefficients (e.g., e = +.0092 in Figure 16) get the same emphasis as fat ones (e.g., f = +.5480 in Figure 16). As a first cut it is often helpful to draw a second diagram that leaves out the arrows for tiny coefficients and exaggerates arrows for the biggest coefficients. What is tiny and what is biggest is a matter of taste. For Figure 16, I decided that anything under .100 was tiny and anything over .200 was big. That gave me Figure 17.

My impression is that the path from father's job to schooling via family income looks promising, but the paths through IQ and grades do not. Although IQ, grades, and schooling seem to form a cluster, the links back to father's job are not strong. It *appears* father's occupation influences schooling more through economic resources than through any influence on academics. Path analysis—working out the value of each path linking father's job and son's schooling—gives a more exact answer. Table 7 displays the paths for father's job and son's schooling.

As Rule 10 promised, the seven indirect paths total .07962, which is within rounding of the .079 we got through effects analysis.

The strongest path, +.039, is, as anticipated, from father's job to family income to schooling. About half of the indirect effect and 20% of the causal is "sheer economics." Although the remaining six effects are

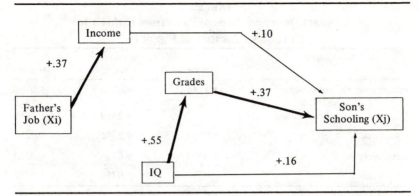

Figure 17 Stronger Relationships in Figure 16

small (none bigger than .01), they add up to .04062, about as much as the "sheer economics." Thus, father's occupation influences college attendance in good part through its contribution to the son's high school academics. (How *that* works is not answerable with our model. Another model with intervening variables—e.g., motivation—to explain our intervenors would be required. There is no end to the possibilities for adding intervening variables. One stops either when the effect is explained or when one is aesthetically satisfied with the level of detail.)

TABLE 7
Decomposition of Paths from Father's Job
to Son's Schooling in Figure 16

Path	Coefficients			Income	IQ	Grades
					Via	
a*h	.3746 * .1041	=	.03900	+	−	−
b*f*j	.0516 * .5480 * .3689	=	.01043	−	+	+
d*j	.0239 * .3689	=	.00882	−	−	+
b*i	.0516 * .1645	=	.00849	−	+	−
a*c*f*j	.3746 * .0845 * .5480 * .3689	=	.00640	+	+	+
a*c*i	.3746 * .0845 * .1645	=	.00521	+	+	−
a*e*j	.3746 * .0092 * .3689	=	.00127	+	−	+
	Total Indirect	=	.07962			
	Direct	=	.1029	−	−	−
	Total	=	.18252			

TABLE 8
Alternate Decompositions of Paths from Father's Job
to Son's Education in Figure 16

Paths	Income	Intervenor IQ	Grades
Father's job to intervenor (times)	+.3746	+.0833	+.0730
Intervenor to son's education	+.1385	+.3667	+.3689
Total	+.0519	+.0305	+.0269
Remainder	+.0277	+.0491	+.0523
Total	+.0796	+.0796	+.0792

Do the data suggest cumulative effects or a long causal chain? A simple answer is found by summing the two step paths (.03900 + .00882 + .00849 = .05631). The effect of father's prestige seem to be mainly cumulative. Reworking the same numbers a la Table 6 gives another perspective (see Table 8).

The middle column in Table 8, for example, says the sum of the paths from father's job to IQ is +.0833, the sum of the paths from IQ to son's education is .3667; their product, +.0305, is the total effect of father's job on son's education routed via IQ; and the total of all the paths connecting father's job and son's education not routed via IQ is .0491.

The three key values (+.0519, +.0305, +.0269) are not very different, but they support the impression that income is the strongest intervenor: 5 of the 8 points of indirect effect operate through income.

Closer scrutiny of the top two rows of Table 8 shows why the three key values are so similar and illustrates a classic principle of path analysis. Income is strongly related to X_i but weakly related to X_j. For IQ and grades, it is the opposite—they are strongly related to X_j and weakly related to X_i. When the terms are multiplied they tend to come out about the same.

The more general point can be called the principle of the weakest link. When working with decimal coefficients such as standardized regression slopes, the value of the path will always be smaller than the value of its smallest link. Even though a path contains strong effects, if one of the links is tiny, the total path effect will be tiny. In our data the strong effect of father's job on income is diluted by the weaker effects of income on schooling, the strong links between IQ, GPA, and grades are diluted by the weak links to father's job. The same idea can be captured by another slogan: It takes two to tango. If you are looking for an intervening variable to explain a correlation, you need one with strong links to *both* Xi and Xj. Beginners in data analysis are often disappointed when they introduce a test variable strongly related to Xi (or Xj) and find the partial correlation is not conspicuously smaller than the bivariate. The answer, of course, is that the test variable didn't have strong links to the *other* variable in the pair to be explained.

A Note on Suppressor Systems: All of the coefficients in Figure 16 are positive, but path analysis works just as well with negative coefficients. Two situations turn up. First, if the system is consistent (see Rule 6) the various signs will cancel one another out automatically. For example, if you reverse the scoring of family income so it becomes family poverty, all its signs would shift from plus to minus; but all its paths would still be positive (e.g., a negative from father's job to poverty times a negative from poverty to son's schooling comes out positive). Second, if the paths from Xi to Xj are inconsistent (some positive, some negative), you will get terms with both plus and minus signs. They will still add up to the total causal effect, no problem there. But is is impossible to divide the total into proportions; to say "25% of the effect is from such and such a path." "Suppressor variables" are an extreme case, as illustrated in the fictitious example in Figure 18.

The specification for Figure 18 says:

a = −.4   Schooling decreases with age (the younger generation is better educated).

b = +.4   Seniority increases with age, net of schooling.

c = 0   Schooling and seniority are unrelated, net of age.

d = +.1   Earnings increase with age, net of schooling and seniority.

e = +.1   Earnings increase with seniority, net of schooling and age.

f = +.5   Earnings increase with schooling, net of age and seniority.

Rule 10 says the causal effect of age on earnings is

$$
\begin{aligned}
\text{Direct} &= +.10 \\
\text{Via Schooling} &= -.20 = -.4 * +.5 \\
\text{Via Seniority} &= \underline{+.04} = +.4 * +.1 \\
&= -.06
\end{aligned}
$$

The total causal effect comprises three terms: +.10 direct, −.20 via schooling, and +.04 via seniority. Their total is −.06. This system would

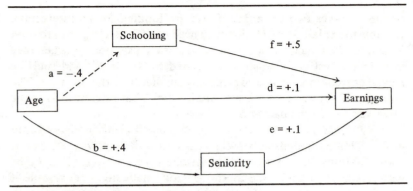

Figure 18 Fictitious Suppressor System

appear to be rather curious if we attacked it via elaboration. We would find a small negative bivariate coefficient of –.06, but when schooling and seniority are controlled, the partial doesn't shrink; instead, it reverses sign and becomes larger. Why? Schooling acts as a suppressor variable: The negative path it creates suppresses the true positive net effect. Such suppression will occur whenever the direct effect has a sign opposite to the sum of the other effects. (Note that in such inconsistent systems effects can still be decomposed into their parts, but the percentages do not add up to 100 in any sensible fashion.)

In sum, when working with regression or other linear model statistics, the indirect part of the causal effect of Xi on Xj can be decomposed exactly into portions, each of which is the product of coefficients along one of the causal paths from Xi to Xj. Such fine-grained analysis is used to sort out the relative strengths of intervening variables and to see whether a causal flow is cumulative or chainlike.

If the system includes variables prior to Xi, Rule 3 says they can produce a causally spurious contribution to the XiXj relationship. Thus, in the Sewell-Hauser data effects analysis told us mother's and father's schoolings added .108 to the relationship between father's job and son's schooling.

Path analysis allows us to decompose the spurious portion into elementary parts so we can see which prior variables are doing what. But the procedure works for only one statistical coefficient (of which I am aware, anyway), the covariance. Since the standardized partial regression coefficient is a special case of the covariance and one seldom uses raw covariances in data analysis, we are really talking about one statistic—the standardized regression coefficient or beta. In this last section of the book possibilities are narrowed considerably. The logic of elaboration and effect analysis applies to any measure of correlation or association, provided some partial or net coefficient can be calculated; the exact calculation of forward paths is appropriate where the "linear model" applies (raw and standardized regression coefficients, percentage differences, which are equivalent to raw regression slopes for 0-1 variables, and dummy variable regression, provided the items are dichotomized). Forward paths can not be decomposed exactly when one uses log linear techniques or dummy variable regression with more than one dummy variable per original item. (When you make more than one dummy variable from an item, you create nasty double-headed arrows among them.) When the goal is an exact decomposition of the causal structures producing spuriousity, only betas work (because one needs a symmetrical coefficient in the linear model family). As, however, they are a very popular statistic, we will proceed with the rationale, despite the earlier promise to talk about logic in general, rather than statistical specifics.

Consider the hypothetical system in Figure 19. A cross-sectional beta may be interpreted as saying, "Cases one sigma apart on the prior variable will average beta sigmas apart on the dependent."
So our specification says cases one sigma apart

—on X1 will be a sigmas apart on X2;

—on X1 will be b sigmas apart on X3 when matched on X2;

—on X2 will be c sigmas apart on X3 when matched on X1.

Now—and this is the whole trick—betas are symmetrical. If the causal effect going forward is, say, .13, the predictive difference going backwards will also be .13. Consequently: Cases one sigma apart on X2 will be a sigma apart on X1; and cases a sigmas apart on X1 will be $a*b$ sigmas apart on X2, even if c were zero.

Aha! The V-structure produced by the prior variables adds $a*b$ spurious points to the correlation. In a three-variable system the spurious contribution of the prior variable, P, is found by multiplying the coefficient for PX_i times the coefficient for PX_j. This is also true for three adjacent variables in a larger system. Thus, in Figure 16, the spurious contribution of IQ on son's grades and son's schooling is .5480 * .1645 = .090146. And the spurious contribution of family income on grades and IQ is .0092 * .0845 = .0007774.

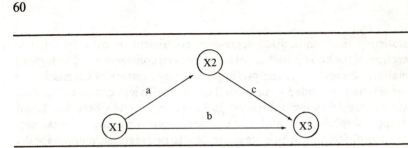

Figure 19   Hypothetical Three-Variable System

With more complex systems, where other variables intervene between the prior and Xi or the prior and Xj, the calculations become very complicated. No advanced math is involved and the theory is the same: We find V-structures that run from the prior to Xi and to Xj and multiply their coefficients, even though on one leg of the V they run backwards. But special rules emerge to prevent double counting, so the procedure is cumbersome. Here are the rules:

(1) Find all forward paths from P to Xi. Write them out using both the coefficients and the numbers of the intervening variables. Thus, in Figure 16 the path from the prior father's job to son's grades through income and IQ would be written a2c3f.

(2) Find all the forward paths from P to Xj using the same notation.

(3) Eliminate all paths in 2 that include Xi as an intervenor. (They link Xi and Xj causally, not spuriously.)

(4) Make a table in which the rows are paths from 1 and the columns are paths from 2 after eliminating those running through Xi.

(5) Consider the cells in the table (each is a combination of paths from P to Xi and P to Xj and hence a potential V-structure). Eliminate any

  (5a) where the same intervening variable appears in both the column and row

  (5b) where the same letter (coefficient) appears in both the column and the row.

(6) For the remaining cells in the table, multiply the row coefficients by column coefficients. Each cell defines a V-structure and the total spurious contribution of P is the sum of the products in these cells.

TABLE 9

Paths from X1 to X2	Paths from X1 to X3	
	b	a2C
a	a*b	—

A simple example and a complex one will illustrate.

First, let's get our result for Figure 19 the hard way. First we find the paths from X1 to X2. That is just *a*. Second, we find the paths from X1 to X3: b + a2c. Now, let's make the table as in Table 9. Because a2c is removed (Step 3) the table has only one cell, a*b.

Now, let's find the spurious contribution of X1 to the X4X5 correlation in Figure 16. The results are shown in Table 10.

TABLE 10

Paths X1 to X4	Paths from X1 to X5			
	g	a2h	b3i	a2c3i
d	g*d	a*h*d	b*i*d	a*c*i*d
a2e	g*a*e	—	b*i*a*e	—
b3f	g*b*f	a*h*b*f	—	—
a2c3f	g*a*c*f	—	—	—

NOTE: — = same letter or number appears in row and column. X1X5 paths d4j, a2e4j, b3f4j, excluded because they run through X4.

For each of the nine lettered cells you can draw a V-structure or path from X1 to X4 and path from X1 to X5 such that no coefficient or variable appears twice. Figure 20 gives two examples. If you work out the coefficient products in each cell and sum them, the result will be the spurious contribution of X1 to the X4X5 correlation. If the system is perfectly ordered, the total spurious correlation will be the sum of the spuriosities contributed by each variable prior to the Xi you are examining.

But that's not quite all. We frequently encounter specifications in which variables at the very beginning (often called "source" or "exogenous variables") have no one-way order but are linked by a curved arrow to indicate ambiguous causation. (This was explained at the very beginning of the book.) Figure 21 illustrates with Sewell-Hauser data.

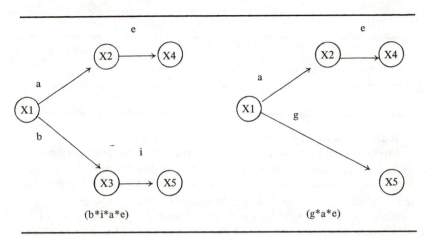

Figure 20   Examples of V-structures for X4X5

If we carry out an effects analysis for X3X4 we get a bivariate of +.448 and a spurious component of .448 – (e = +.3746) = .0734. Seven points of the relationship between father's job and family income are spurious, due to the influence of parental educations.

Applying our spuriousity principles, we find the contributions as follows:

Father's schooling = .3971 ∗ .1152 = .0457 = a ∗ c
Mother's schooling = .0805 ∗ .0796 = .0064 = b ∗ d

We can account for .0521 (.0457 + .0064) of the .0734 spurious effect by the simple forward influences of parental schoolings. The remainder, .0213, is too large to be rounding. It is produced, not by a particular prior variable, but by the correlation between them.

To see how it works, let us introduce a hypothetical prior variable, PO, which produces the correlation between parental educations. Obviously, we do not know the sizes of its two coefficients, but from the principles of spuriousity, we know their product is .520. So, let's take any two numbers that multiply to .520, say .800 and .650. (It doesn't make any difference which numbers you choose and you can get the same results with abstract letters, but a little false specificity may help keep things straight.) Now, let's work out the contribution of PO to the X3X4 correlation. Applying the procedures explained above, the table looks

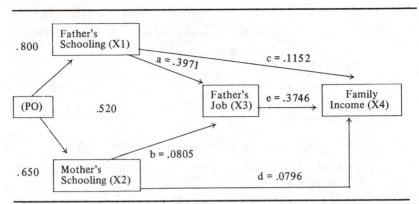

Figure 21   Four Variables from Sewell-Hauser Study

like that in Table 11. Since .80*65 equals .52, it simplifies to: .52 (a*d + b*c) = .52 (.00927 + .0316) = .0213. The result, .0213, is, of course, the missing part.

Graphically, effects produced by correlated source pairs look like a letter "u." Figure 22 illustrates.

When X_i and X_j are farther down the line the forward paths have more links, but the structures are the same—the bottom of the u is the correlation between the priors and the structure has two arms hooked onto the priors, one running to X_i and one running to X_j. (Alternatively, you can think of them as V-structures running from a hypothetical prior-prior that produced the correlation between the two source variables.)

These calculations not only keep things tidy by assuring us everything adds up, they define an interesting causal process—the ability of pairs of source variables to influence a correlation because something tends to line *them* up. Mother's and father's characteristics are an important sociological example. The tendency for husbands and wives to be similar on a variety of social characteristics (sociologists call this "homogamy") has a definite impact on other relationships in models of parental influence.

In summary, when working with standardized partial regression coefficients in a loop free model, the correlation between any X_i and X_j (except X_1 and X_2) can be exactly decomposed into

—a direct effect,

—indirect effects associated with paths connecting them,

TABLE 11

| | Paths from P0 to X4 | |
Paths from P0 to X3	.80 (X1) c	.65 (X2) d
.80 (X1) a	–	.80*65*a*d
.65 (X2) b	.80*65*b*c	–

—spurious effects associated with particular prior variables,
—spurious effects associated with the correlations between pairs of source variables.

In practice, one seldom attempts complete decompositions in systems with more than three or four variables, but an understanding of the principles involved is an invaluable tool for the analyst. The seasoned data analyst continually plays the intellectual game of asking what underlying structures would produce the bivariate relationships in the data and then makes the multivariate runs to see whether the guess is right. Path analysis is rare as an actual statistical calculation, but it is built into the thinking of the experienced research worker.

3. THE COSTS OF BEING WRONG

Causal order is central to multivariate analysis. We cannot even begin estimation until we have specified a causal order. The numbers we get for our relationships may jump around considerably or even reverse sign, depending on which variables are introduced as controls.

At the same time, there is no magic statistical device for telling us whether the specification is correct. We can advance commonsense arguments, but it is difficult to give airtight justifications for each pair. It therefore behooves us to consider what damage may be done when we are wrong.

First, let us consider control variables. Assuming X_i and X_j are ordered correctly, what happens if we are wrong about the position of the other variables?

(A) *If any control variables are actually consequent to X_j we can do ourselves considerable damage.*

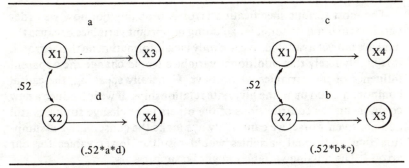

Figure 22   U-Structures in Figure 21

If a control variable really comes after Xj, it can have no causal effect on any variable anywhere in the system. Yet if we introduce it as a variable, we may erroneously change the coefficients for all the other variables in the system. Never control on a consequent variable.

(B) *Providing Xts are not consequent to Xj, errors in order have no effect on direct relationships or Lazarsfeldian elaboration.*

Rule 7 tells us that we control *all* prior and intervening variables when estimating an arrow, whatever their exact place in the chain. Therefore, we will get exactly the same direct effect with any ordering of the Xts—providing none are consequent to Xj.

(C) *Effect analysis is insensitive to order among priors and order among intervenors.*

If we have six intervening variables whose internal order is hopelessly scrambled, we will get exactly the same results in our effect analysis whatever order we use, provided they are all intervening.

This rule can be extremely useful as it allows us to treat whole classes of variables without worrying about their internal order. For example, if we wish to know whether political opinions explain the correlation between Xi and Xj, we can look at the correlation between Xi and Xj controlling for a variety of opinions without having to worry about which opinion influences which.

(D) *Absent variables might do anything.*

The most serious specification error is probably not how we order variables in our data set; it is excluding important variables because the data are not yet available. We not only lack information on their arrows, it is highly likely that additional variables would change the apparent influence of the variables we do have. Generally speaking, the causal components add up to the bivariate relationships. If we introduce a new component, the contributions of the others must change so things still add up. Even worse, we cannot always make the conservative assumption that additional variables would result in lower values for our arrows. The missing variables might be suppressors.

Perhaps the most important step in interpreting data is to give serious consideration to plausible variables, not present in the analysis or even in the data set, that might have chains of relationships to the X_i and X_j in question.

At the same time you should remember that the X_iX_j relationship is not hostage to any old X_t. If you can plausibly argue that a missing X_t is unrelated to X_i *or* unrelated to X_j, you can ignore it. Thus, as we saw earlier, there is no reason to worry about excluding sex as a control when looking at the effect of race on something.

Now, let us consider problems of ordering X_i and X_j themselves. Provided we can work out proper controls, X_iX_j order is not as severe a problem as one might imagine. If, of course, we confuse section a and section b of Figure 1, we will have a hopeless mess. And if we have X_i and X_j reversed, we will have a disaster, because our causal reasoning will be totally wrong. But such an extreme goof is unlikely. When an arrow is really one-way, one has to be pretty stupid to get it *backwards*. The most likely error is where X_i and X_j form a loop but we assume a one-way effect. Thus:

we think:

$$a = .62$$
$$X_i \longrightarrow X_j$$

but it's really:

$$b = .50$$
$$X_i \rightleftarrows X_j$$
$$a = .40$$

Under our specification it appears that when Xi goes up one unit, Xj goes up .62 units; but in truth, when Xi goes up one unit, Xj goes up .5, and .4 of this is fed back to Xi, which then raises Xj a bit, which then, and so on.

Loop theory (see Heise, 1975) tells us the correct result is

$$XiXj = \frac{a}{1 - a * b} = \frac{.5}{1 - (.5 * .4)} \ ^{l=}.62$$

In this example the real answer is .5, but we got .62 through misspecification. An error, but not a catastrophe.

More to the point, our .62 is the correct answer for how much Xj will have changed after the loop effect has settled down, following a unit change in Xi.

In other words, when the only misspecification is treating Xi and Xj as one-way rather than a loop, we get the correct answer for the total direct effect, but we miss the causal mechanism by which it operates.

In sum, specification errors are important. It is possible to obtain results that are statistically impeccable but totally erroneous by leaving out key variables or making egregious errors in order. True enough, but you should keep this all in perspective, bearing in mind the following counter-principles:

(1) There are very few "whopper" effects in social science. The variables you left out might make things stronger or weaker but if something had a massive correlation with your Xi and Xj, you would probably have heard about it.

(2) For some important questions (e.g., elaboration) most specification errors have minor or no negative effects.

(3) You can and should use the principles of causal logic to work out for yourself—before your critics get at you—potential sources of specification error and exactly what damage they might or might not do to you.

4. SUMMARY

Even a short book can be boiled down. This one centers on three ideas: (1) Causal analysis in social research depends on assumptions about causal direction; (2) these assumptions depend on empirical beliefs about how the world works. No statistical routine can give you the answers; (3) the assumptions are not arbitrary or whimsical. They involve a set of specific concepts and principles, summarized below:

(1) Ordering X and Y

Run the arrow from X to Y if

(a) Y starts after X freezes,

(b) X is linked to an earlier step in a well-known sequence,

(c) X never changes and Y sometimes changes,

(d) X is more stable, harder to change, or more fertile.

(2) System order

If there is a path starting from X and returning to it without retracing any steps, X and all the variables on the path form a loop.

Variables in a loop have no order.

(3) Spurious association

If a prior variable has a causal path to the independent variable and a causal path to the dependent variable, it will contribute a statistical association between them that is causally spurious.

(4) Polarities

Reversing poles for one variable reverses the signs of each of its relationships.

Reversing poles for both variables leaves the sign of their relationship unchanged.

(5) The sign rule

The sign of a path is given by multiplying the signs of its arrows.

(or)

A path of nonzero arrows will be positive unless it contains an odd number of negative arrows.

(6) Consistency

A system is inconsistent if at least one pair of variables has both positive and negative signs among its direct, indirect, and spurious effects. Otherwise, it is consistent.

If a system is consistent, all negative arrows can be eliminated by reversing polarities.

(7) Control

When estimating a direct effect of X_i on X_j, control all prior and intervening variables—that is, control all variables not consequent to X_j.

In multiple regression, regress each variable on all its predecessors.

(8) Explanation

A test variable, X_t, explains X_iX_j when the X_iX_j bivariate is nonzero and the X_iX_j partial, controlling for X_t, is zero or trivially small.

To explain a positive correlation, look for X_ts where X_tX_i and X_tX_j have the same sign.

To explain a negative correlation, look for X_ts where X_tX_i and X_tX_j have opposite signs.

Unless X_t is related to both X_i and X_j it is a poor candidate for explainer.

(9) Effects Analysis

In addition to the XY bivariate (A) and the direct XY effect (C), calculate (B), the causal effect, by controlling prior variables only. Then find the spurious component (A-B) and the indirect portion due to intervening variables (B-C).

(10) Paths

In a linear system the total causal effect of X_i on X_j is the sum of the values of all the paths from X_i to X_j.

NOTES

1. A variable is fertile if it has a variety of obvious effects, other than Y. The argument is that a variable that affects lots of things is more likely to affect Y than a variable that is not known to affect anything much. Thus, one can think of many possible sociological consequences of changing one's spouse, but one is pressed to think of any sociological consequences of changing one's brand of toothpaste.

2. If Black were scored $-$, we'd get the same conclusion with $XtXi = -$ and $XtXj = +$.

REFERENCES

ALWIN, D. F. and R. M. HAUSER (1975) "The decomposition of effects in path analysis." American Sociological Review 40: 37-47.

BERRY, W. D. (1984) Nonrecursive Causal Models. Beverly Hills, CA: Sage.

BLAU, P. and O. D. DUNCAN (1967) The American Occupational Structure. New York: John Wiley.

DAVIS, J. A. (1975) "Analyzing contingency tables with linear flow graphs: D systems," pp. 111-145 in D. Heise (ed.) Sociological Methodology 1976. San Francisco: Jossey-Bass.

FINNEY, J. M. (1972) "Indirect effects in path analysis." Sociological Methods and Research 1: 175-186.

HEISE, D. (1975) Causal Analysis. New York: John Wiley.

TAYLOR, D. G. (1983) "Analyzing qualitative data," pp. 547-612 in P. Rossi (ed.) Handbook of Survey Research. New York: Academic Press.

JAMES A. DAVIS is Professor of Sociology and Master of Winthrop House, Harvard University, and Research Associate at the National Opinion Research Center (NORC), University of Chicago. He has been involved in NORC survey research for 30 years and, since 1972, has served as Principal Investigator of its General Social Survey. Professor Davis is the author of 35 academic articles and 6 books. His undergraduate training was in journalism at Northwestern University.

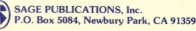

Quantitative Applications in the Social Sciences

(a Sage University Papers Series)

$6.50 each

SAGE PUBLICATIONS, INC.

P.O. BOX 5084

NEWBURY PARK, CALIFORNIA 91359—9924